Good Boss, Bad Boss

A primer for those in a leadership role seeking advice and everyday ideas and methodology in the ethical and humane treatment of your teams and the operation of your business.

Terry L. Werner

Dedication

For **Kim** - the perfect Assistant, beyond equal Peer, and most importantly, a wonderful Friend.

For **Craig**, **Bill**, **Karen**, **Matt**, **Jeff**, **Jochen**, and **Lee** - for demonstrating what a leader should/can be.

For my **Family**, that tolerated my incessant need to share myself with my work "family" - all too often at their expense.

Table of Contents

Foreword

I first met Terry almost forty years ago. Sounds crazy as I type that. Way back then, he was my manager at a large retail pharmacy. Our personalities immediately clicked, and it didn't take long to see how well we would work together. I actually think we could finish each other's sentences! I knew and understood what he wanted and how he wanted it done. I was attending college at the time for something totally unrelated to management. Watching Terry work and lead his team made me begin to wonder if this was the path I wanted to take instead. He so effectively uses all of the techniques and ideas in this book and taught me so much about what it would take to become a good manager. He had a way of seamlessly being direct with very high expectations without making his employees feel belittled or in any way lacking the ability to do their job effectively. I became his assistant and learned a great deal from him over the next few years. He not only became my mentor but also a very good friend. I am proud and very happy to say that it has lasted for many years now! Our lives and careers moved on for a time and then we once again, many years later found ourselves working together. He hired me to work for him at a worldwide print center and I began learning from him once again! Knowing our history and the fact that I was once before his assistant, he put me on a fast track to move up in the company. It wasn't long after that I got the opportunity to manage my own store. Terry has always had confidence in me. With his guidance and my observation of his leadership style, he helped me with the opportunity to pursue my career. Effective managers help employees stay motivated to do their best work. They work to make them feel valued, supported and empowered. These are all characteristics of a good leader. Terry had these and many more. I have witnessed and been a part of his managerial style over many years. Yes, customers are always first and foremost, but your employees are crucial to the success of your business. He knew this and always treated his workers with respect, making sure they had the tools, knowledge and autonomy to do their jobs and do them well. I was moved and honored when Terry asked me to read his book to see if it had any merit at all as a tool and guide for others. He actually said, "will this be useful or is it completely trivial and so basic that a caveman could've done it!" After reading it my response was that I loved the fact that the book is simple, direct and to the point. Being a good manager and an effective leader isn't easy and not everyone will be good at it. Some will be wildly successful, some tragically inept while others will fall somewhere in between. There's no secret to success. However, I believe that Terry has outlined a great recipe to follow so one can be an effective, strong leader. He gives you a guideline that will offer you tools, ideas and methods that will help you become the manager you want to become. He does this by sharing some of his own personal experiences to help show how and why these ways will work. I have seen firsthand the value of utilizing the ideas Terry has put forth in the following pages. Again, there are no guarantees of success, but if you are looking to better yourself and be a more effective manager or leader in any business, I truly believe what Terry has laid out will prove to be exceedingly beneficial toward your success. His words are honest, sincere and, in my opinion, invaluable to your career. This is not a one size fits all narrative, but I believe there will be something new and outside of the box for many readers. Maybe you will read parts and realize where you may be going awry. Learning from mistakes is part of this journey as well. You may just get that "Ah ha" moment when you read some or many of the ideas that follow! Regardless of where you may be in your leadership journey, it is sure to point you in the right direction.

Kim Marie Heburn

Introduction

In 2021, I stepped away from a 40 plus year career in business management. Sadly, the circumstances of my "retirement" weren't as I had planned but sometimes life throws unexpected curveballs your way and you're forced to swing at a pitch that lands in the dirt. Nonetheless, I am now happy after 18 months of getting adjusted to this new reality. In keeping busy, I've rekindled an old desire to do some creative writing. That inspiration to this point had become a "someday when I have the time" project since college. Well, guess what? I have the time now and I've rejuvenated the old creative juices and dusted off the shelf where the Great American novel will rest once, I've written it. While semi-isolated during the pandemic of 2020, I wrote an autobiography for the reading pleasure (?) of my children so they can perhaps figure out why I think and act the way I do. Good luck with that! I seriously doubt that Stephen King should be watching his back, but I am happy to be making the attempt. I have started that novel, and it now sits undisturbed on my computer desktop since June of 2022. Stagnant and resting at the 14833 word mark, while the characters within are aging as I write this. I keep telling myself that I need to resume writing it and feel fairly comfortable that someday I will pick at those keys again and move their stories along in their timeline. I await the proverbial inspiration to strike. Thus far, the dust still settles on that tale.

An inspiration befell me one evening while pondering my situation. Somewhat fondly, I reminisced about those I've encountered in the workplace and subsequent side-gatherings resulting from trainings, travels and meetings. I also reflected upon the plethora of the self-help books, instructor-led courses, conference calls and a myriad of information presented to me (and others) throughout the years with the intention of making us better managers of business and of the people in our employ. So many catch phrases, popular jargon euphemisms combined with witticisms and an overabundance of acronyms. Every session or course had takeaways that rattled in your head like an earworm you can't escape. One large corporation I was employed by actually had a printed dictionary of the acronyms that were used within the jargon of the employees. As technology changed, so did the acronyms that represented the tasks and equipment to perform them. Just imagine the impact this had on the new hires during their first few weeks trying to blend in and assimilate. It certainly wasn't limited to that particular business as I had encountered the same types of internal-speak with every organization.

The overly competitive challenge dominating American businesses since the 1970's was favorable to the careers of some and devastating to others less talented. I not only survived, but managed to climb my way up the corporate rungs of the organizations that hired me and succeeded in becoming a respected member of middle management. Why was I successful and, even more importantly, well-liked and respected? I still have contacts from the very beginnings of my career that are long-term friends and acquaintances. Why did those relationships survive the termination of the professional relationships? After consideration, I began to believe that instead of continuation of the dust-gathering novel, perhaps I should attempt to pen a business orientated tome that addresses a few of these questions. Those small, inconsequential and intangible actions that can take an everyday manager-employee relationship and transform it into a bond that exists outside and beyond the end of the complexities of the industrial realm.

On the following pages, I have outlined what I believe to be the basics for the successful business manager in terms of ethical behavior and interpersonal interactions with those who report to them directly or indirectly. I've also discussed actions the successful leader can and should take to ensure that a healthy environment exists to incubate desirable performance by those who report to that leader. There is nothing Earthshattering here and quite possibly deemed obvious and even second nature to some experienced managers. Maybe you missed a few of these tidbits along the way and perhaps the principles learned in The One Minute Manager have disappeared from your persona or have never sat in the office chair next to you offering advice.

Reflecting upon the various management positions I've held since my very first supervisory role while attending college in the early 1980's and continuing through the last 29 years with a world leading shipping/retail company, I realized one thing remained constant throughout my 40 plus year career. It was the ability to interact and direct teams of Co-Workers, Teammates, Employees (whatever your term of choice), to realize company and individual goals and achieve initiatives we were either directed to institute or were self-driven to conquer. Although almost every task, goal and initiative was for the sole purpose of furthering the financial success of the parent company and deliver better ROI to the shareholders, the methods in which those objectives are realized fall upon the shoulders of the direct manager who is required to provide the training and daily directives and follow-up to ensure the end results meet the objective desired. Those same managers are most often given a general guideline as to the desired outcomes, suggested training methodology, timeframes, resources and often consequences of failure for both the underling and sometimes even the direct manager themselves. The most important element, however, is missing from the slide deck. Very little or non-existent is the succinct "how to" instruction for direct one-on-one involvement of manager with employee. Missing are the definitive interactions that will determine whether you succeed or fail in your mission as a business leader and director of multi-member teams. So many books have been written about how to set objectives, determine goals and measure their achievement that bookstores and office shelves are teeming with them. Many volumes have also been composed on the topic of how to treat people and set your own limits on those interpersonal relationships. When the idea presented itself to me that I should try my hand at writing such a book, I wondered what would make this different from the rest. Why would anyone wish to read this little self-indulgent retelling of some of my exploits and the lessons learned wherein? I hope that answer would make itself evident once you have reviewed the ideas presented. As stated, they are not revolutionary nor Earth shaking. There is no quantum physics theory. No magic bullet. No life-changing line that you tack up on your refrigerator. But maybe, just maybe there is that proverbial light that switched on as you were reading. Perhaps you can now see that you might be able to get through to that one co-worker or that group from "that division" that until now has been very aloof and distant in their dealings with you or your department. Perhaps you can try a different tactic now to reach them and bridge that gap. Nothing ventured, nothing gained and maybe you need a previously untried approach. Most businesses offer internal trainings to their management teams and high potential team members they hope to one day promote into that role but not all cookie-cutter type trainings fit all types of management styles.

I've worked with the "Type A" managers through the "Type Z" and the one thing they all have in common is that each of them has learned most of if not all their "skill set" from someone who mentored them prior to being let loose to lead others. This is not the best method in which to raise a new leader unless there is additional exposure to those that offer a different perspective and approach to the methodology required to be successful. Einstein stated that doing the same thing over and over again and expecting different results was the definition of insanity. That same principle applies to managers who try to use the exact same approach with everyone when interacting with the individuals on their assigned teams. My hope is that the ideas laid out on the remaining pages of this book might present some new ideas and approaches to the day-to-day interactions with those you work with as a peer, direct as a supervisor or maybe they just live in another room of your home or frequent your favorite coffee house. You have made many attempts to break through to them but until this moment they have presented a challenge to you when you are face-to-face. Before you give up on making that connection, try a renewed perspective on their vantage point. Perhaps the obstacles to understanding are your own. As I stated, nothing ventured, nothing gained. What can be gained, however, may be beyond your wildest dreams and untapped productivity and growth may be only a gesture away.

In the end, I ask myself if I believe I had a successful career, and my honest answer is found in the relationships developed while being the leader of untold amazing individuals. As Clarence Oddbody (AS2) states at the end of It's a Wonderful Life, "no man is a failure who has friends."

Definitions of Leadership by Different Authors

R. W. Griffin defines, "Leadership can be defined as the ability to influence others."

Peter Drucker defines, "The only definition of a leader is someone who has followers."

According to Keith Davis, "Leadership is the process of encouraging and helping others to work enthusiastically toward objectives."

According to Van Fleet, "Leadership is an influence process directed at shaping the behavior of others."

John Maxwell states, "Leadership is influence, nothing more, nothing less."

C.I. Bernard defines, "Leadership is the quality of behavior of the individuals whereby they guide people or their activities in organized efforts."

According to Warren Bennis, "leadership is a function of knowing yourself, having a vision that is well communicated, building trust among colleagues, and taking effective action to realize your own leadership potential."

According to Koontz and O'Donnell, "Leadership is the process of influencing people so that they will strive willingly towards the achievement of group goals."

U.S. Airforce defines, "Leadership is the art of influencing and directing people in such a way that will win their obedience, confidence, respect, and loyal cooperation in achieving common objectives."

Bernard Keys and Thomas defined, "Leadership is the process of influencing and supporting others to work enthusiastically towards achieving objectives."

According to George R. Terry, "Leadership is a relationship in which one person influences others to work together willingly on related tasks to attain what the leader desires."

Adeoye Mayowa defines, "Leadership is the ability to evaluate and or forecast a long term plan or policy and influence the followers towards the achievement of the said strategy."

According to Charles Handy (1992), "A leader shapes and shares a vision which gives point to the work of others."

Hosking said, "Leaders are those who consistently make effective contributions to social order, and who are expected and perceived to do so."

Northouse defines, "Leadership is a process whereby an individual influences a group of individuals to achieve a common goal."

According to Hemphill & Coons, "Leadership is the behavior of an individual when he is directing the activities of a group toward a shared goal."

According to Buchannan and Huczynski, "Leadership is a social process in which one individual influences the behavior of others without the use of threat or violence

Be Business Ready

When you unlock that front door at opening time, you and your team must be ready to greet and treat that first customer as you would a customer who enters your establishment when the mechanism of your normalcy has been running smoothly for hours on end. That first customer or client must never feel that your attention is distracted by other tasks or the lack of staffing. No genuine excuse can be conjured up to provide anything less than the expected interaction. That expectation the customer carries in the door is the least experience they should realize. Your directive as the business manager is to exceed every expectation that a client enters with. If you cannot or will not provide this experience every time, stop reading here, ask for a refund, find employment as a lone worker in some remote area, and never look back.

Sadly, today, post-pandemic, we have settled for mediocrity in our businesses. Kiosks replacing the frontline service representative, online ordering, DoorDash, instacart, etc., have allowed the service and fast-food industries to surrender exceptional customer service for proclaimed hands-free, touch-free, sterile curbside interactions. They have played upon our fears of COVID-19 to further the opportunity to lower staffing and eliminate the need for exceptional customer service to retain and grow their customer base. I was a manager for a top fast-food company in the 1980s for a few years, and the difference between that era and what passes for their business model today is astounding. I credit that time in my early management career with many of the talents and philosophies I embody. I have relied upon them my entire life in business situations and everyday life. Most notable is the sense of urgency. I don't know if that can be taught or if it is a naturally occurring trait in some humans that can be nurtured and developed until it becomes dominant. Regardless, it is something that is so incredibly valuable to a manager or leader of teams or anyone who wishes to get tasks completed without having to rely upon alarms, lists, or a supervisor looking over your shoulder. The manager possessing that sense will know instinctively if that front door is ready to open and allow business to commence. They will have already performed a walk-through of their location to ensure everything is in place and the team is prepared to hit the ground running. Nothing gets overlooked because the routine won't allow it. It may be a type of "Spidey sense." Still, they know when the fabric is weak in some area and will not withstand the pressures the business will bear upon it and have already gotten the ball rolling on the repair or adjustment that will prevent that all-important figure, the customer, from ever seeing or detecting the chink in the operation that was so discreetly avoided. The manager or leader who reacts to the potential disaster instead of preventing it is lost in the battle to control the ever-engulfing fire that will spread and burn the business. They will need to rebuild not only the business but also the reassurance and commitment of their teams to go back into battle the following day, as well as the confidence of the client or customer who witnessed the burnout. Some serious events have the consequences of losing employees and customers forever. That ounce of prevention can be attributed to that sense of urgency.

I also learned the concept of image and brand from that same organization. If you agree to take upon the role of leader or manager, you must also agree to represent whole-heartedly that organization that you have signed on with. You simply must "represent." Suppose, however, you discover the corporation or business entity is not as upstanding and ethical as you believed.

In that case, I do not espouse deceiving your teams to forward the agenda of that agency. If anything, find a better opportunity and move on. I had that experience once when I was recruited away from managing a leading pharmacy chain location by the owner of a 40-location dry cleaning chain, which turned out to have some extremely unethical business practices; I was astounded and appalled by the policies and social views of the owner and refused to abide by some of his directives that violated not only State and Federal laws but my self-respect. After a 10-month tenure of head-butting, we parted ways, and he gave my position to a relative in need of employment. Lesson learned.

The fast-food giant I learned from taught me about brand awareness and perception of that image. It doesn't matter what we think of the company we represent. The only opinion that does matter is that of the customer or client. They taught me this in a most unexpected manner. Every half hour or so, one of the managers on shift was required to walk a "travel path." This consisted of walking around the dining area to check for cleanliness, followed by a close inspection of each restroom, and then having a team member immediately perform whatever maintenance was needed to return those areas to the standards that existed for every area within the location. The same was conducted in the food production areas whenever a lull occurred. Once the manager finished these quick inspections, they did not simply return to their duties overseeing the area of the location they were supervising that day. Instead, they left the building and took a predetermined route around the entire building and area immediately adjacent to the neighborhood. The primary purpose of this routine was to pick up every piece of trash that contained the business's name, the image of its logo, known representation or caricature, or in any way could be construed as remnants of a visit to our business. It simply wasn't acceptable to allow the perception that the organization contributed to endangering or polluting the environment and sullying our neighborhoods. Overflowing trash barrels were unheard of in our parking lot. Today, you can hardly deposit trash in the cans located near businesses as they are most often teeming with trash and have small piles at the base of the receptacle that wouldn't fit. I've been a trash picker ever since. This same habit is still used on my front lawn and neighboring lawns. If it reflects upon my house, I will pick it up so our household image isn't blemished. What a wonderful ideology – if only everyone picked up the trash instead of tossing it out the car window when leaving the drive-thru! Perception is reality.

There were standards regarding speed of service as well. The time was measured from when a car would arrive at the speaker in the drive-thru, and acknowledgment began the transaction. Speed of acknowledgment was measured, as was the length of the entire time it took before they pulled away from the window with their hot and correctly fulfilled order in hand. The entire transaction time was less than a few minutes. Sadly, I lost or discarded my little pocket guide listing all the standards, but I know it was less than 2 minutes from the speaker to "Thank you – come again." I dug into those statistics and found that a location functioning extremely well would average 25 seconds per order and serve upwards of 144 cars in an hour! Today, you can wait much longer to receive the food you ordered online or at a kiosk. There is no personal interaction. If you are able to speak to anyone, it's minimal, impersonal, or aggressive. You aren't greeted. There is no sense of urgency or concern regarding your perception of the service rendered. And there is certainly no "Cheers" atmosphere where everyone knows your name. There is a more significant concern about orders being picked up by a delivery driver and what can only be described as general chaos at the unstaffed front counter – provided that there is still a counter. The "Founder" who insisted upon service excellence must be nearing China with all the grave turning he must be doing.

Let me relate a quick story. In December of this year (2023), my wife and I were in southern Indiana one evening as a layover on a Louisville area trip. It was getting late, and we stopped at a chain Mexican fast-food location to grab a quick bite before heading to our hotel. We were just one of two groups in the restaurant lobby. The other group had at least one member who was an off-duty employee of the establishment. We learned this because he and his compadres found engaging those "working" behind the counter in crude and extremely loud conversation was necessary and perfectly normal. There were at least eight people in the kitchen area, and their music, yelling, and otherwise, pleasant interactions with one another were only interrupted by a patron's arrival through the restaurant doors or the drive-thru window. I say interruption, but only those tasked with interacting with the patrons directly ceased their antics as the rest continued boisterously. I cringed at what I saw and heard. The tables in the lobby hadn't been cleaned, the floor was a mess, and the areas around the self-serve soda area were poorly stocked and instead dirty looking. In my mind, I formulated the idea that surely no manager is on duty, as they wouldn't allow such behavior.
I was correct, it would seem, as shortly after we began to eat our meal, a car came flying into the parking lot and a young woman entered the building. As she entered, almost all of the team shouted, "Ashley!" "Ashley's here!" "Well," I thought, "Things will get whipped into shape." Ashley moved behind the front counter, stood facing the dining area, and released the loudest burp I had ever heard. She then muttered

something about not "remembering I ate that" and joined in the overall din of the kitchen staff. Crude, rude, and unprofessional, but more importantly, the perception of that brand will forever be the reality in our minds.

This change in business philosophy saddens me. I recently had an experience that was such a dramatic example of this new method of allowing the chickens to rule the roost and set the tone for your business. My wife and I decided on our way home from a day trip to stop at a major fast-food chain to pick up an ice cream treat for our son, who had been on dog duty all day while we were gone. We pulled into line at the drive-thru at roughly 15 minutes past 7 PM and were third in line to the speaker. After nearly five minutes, we were next in line to the speaker and about to place our simple one-item order and get back on our way. Out of nowhere, a person emerged from behind our vehicle and approached the driver's side window, which was open, awaiting to be acknowledged by the speaker. This person was almost recognizable as an employee of the business as he had what looked like a partial uniform and was carrying a visor with the company logo - twirling it around a finger. He approached our car, halted about ten feet away, and made a simple announcement. "We are closing now. You'll have to come back some other time." He then left the area and headed for his parked vehicle. We sat there stunned. There was no explanation, no offers of apologies, no personalization or ownership of the business. Nothing, not even "kiss my ass!" The manager in me was dumbfounded and, flustered and uncomprehending. The customer in me was startled, disappointed, and disbelieving, not to mention pissed off. I spent the remainder of our trip home recounting to my wife the things he "should" have done. My team member would have approached the car, announced we were closing, and inquired as to what we would like to order as we would represent the last order of their day. He would wait until we were served before actually pulling the plug. There would also be apologies for being forced to close our services outside the posted hours of operation. We would also be thanked for our business and asked to return. There would be adequate signage at the drive-thru speaker and front and side doors explaining such and apologizing for the unforeseen inconveniences.

Alas and alack, this is what passes for service in this new age. I, for one, mourn for the days when the customer was the desirable entity and not the "problem" they represent today to the staff that populate modern businesses. A business where they have fallen on the sword of always being "short-staffed" and have lackadaisical attitudes toward fulfilling the implicit contract that exists between server and patron. Ignoring the once-established expectation of treatment once the front door chimes and announces the arrival of a new guest. Being ready for business has a much deeper meaning than merely looking as a business whose entrance is unlocked and somewhat inviting. At its core, there must be the desire, diligence, commitment, and thirst or even lust for an unwavering extraordinary experience of satisfaction bordering upon the delight of the client who graces your doorway. Nothing else will do if you genuinely wish to be successful in your business endeavors in which a customer frequents your establishment to consume your wares or partake of your services. Even in this day of retail saturation and pop-up eateries where most experiences are non-noteworthy, the adage still applies. If you cannot provide this experience for your clientele, someone else will, and you will be left holding the clearance sale and going out of business liquidation when they cease their connection with you. Customers will forgive you a time or two when a relationship exists but will be lost if they have been left underwhelmed by your demonstrated acceptance of subpar performance from your staff or teams.

As Harry Truman admonished, "The buck stops here," nothing could be more accurate when placing blame or showering accolades on the performance of teams, departmental groups, or staff. The management style you bring to the table will ultimately be reflected in the achievement or utter failure of those you lead. How you conduct yourself and the image you present to that team will be the model from which they learn and ultimately adapt their behavior to reflect. Furthermore, the methods used in interpersonal relationships and interactions with the individuals within those groups will determine the amount of respect and adherence to the stated goals and objectives you outline and, thus, the degree of success you (they) achieve. So often today, I overhear self-proclaimed leaders lamenting that they should command a higher salary at the point of entry into the business world, demand instant respect and gripe about having to work an evening or weekend shift. If that is you, then move on to another career. Leaders must earn their due. A true leader expects to put in long hours, sacrifice weekends, evenings and holidays with loved ones until they climb their way up through devotion, diligence and plain old hard work.

In the following chapters, I will outline the methodologies and practices that I found critical in my leadership of many teams during my career. I will discuss ideas of engagement and practices learned from development I gleaned through first-hand experience, the multitude of trainings I attended and delivered throughout that timeframe, and most importantly, those lessons learned from the observation of other management personnel either in levels above me, my direct peers, or those trying to find their way and management style. There are also many lessons learned through negative experiences at the hands of these same groups.

I'm reminded of a business consultant that I had the pleasure of meeting several times at company-sponsored training seminars in the 1990s. He was a short, stout man with a distinct Baltic accent who specialized in bringing a sense of passion, zeal, and excitement into his presentation to convey and generate that same excitement in the attendees so that they might take it back to their specific locations and thus energize their teams to drive increased success. If you met him, you would certainly never forget him. He would single out one of the attendees and quiz them about their particular branch and the practices they followed. He would allow them to speak for a few minutes and maybe ask a few follow-up questions before declaring he would open a location across the street from them and proceed to "put you out of business." He would list the different things he would do to attract their customers away and hopefully light a fire of increased awareness under that attendee who might, in turn, see their own business through the eyes of their customers and perhaps modify their behaviors to prevent such an attack by a competitor. A true leader will find and establish those "barriers to entry" so they don't see themselves with dwindling customer loyalty but continuously innovate to prevent such an occurrence.

Set Them Up To Succeed

Anyone who has spent any amount of tenure as a leader, especially those in retail management, will attest to the proven fact that it is much, much easier to retain experienced, dedicated, and diligent employees than it is to recruit, hire, and train new folks to replace those that have left your team. I will look at methods and practices you can use to help retain those longer-term workers, but first, I wish to tackle the best practices surrounding the introduction of the new hire team member when they come on board and join your team. Nothing could be of greater importance than how that newly hired person is introduced to those already entrenched in the day-to-day activities of your organization.

When possible, an announcement should be made before the starting date regarding hiring a new member and some of that person's credentials. With that action, there is no degree of "shock" when they walk in on that first day and are paraded before the other constituents of their new coworkers. Assistant managers or department heads should be included in the screening, interviewing, and hiring process whenever possible so that they, too, have a more significant stake in the success of the new talent and perhaps will take a more active role in ensuring that success. The recruit will have a more dynamic starting point with these additional advocates. They believe they are already a known entity to several amongst the management and feel more at ease when integrated into the remaining staff members. Only a sheer narcissist would desire to be paraded before a group of people they aren't known to and be the subject of scrutiny and perhaps even ridicule or gossip. But this is precisely what happens to most new hires that enter an organization. They are often the subjects of rumor, gossip, scuttlebutt, and gossipy fabrication. For many, it becomes overwhelming, and, in some cases, they never return from their very first lunch break and opt instead to try their hand elsewhere because this new environment is perceived to be unfriendly, unwelcoming, and most undoubtedly standoffish. The sad part is that with most of these quick-termed employees, much went into the screening and hiring process, and the apparent talents discovered from those interviews most likely would have brought additional resources to the team they were joining. All those recruiting efforts are now for naught. Everybody loses. The recruit that is now in need of seeking employment elsewhere, the hiring team that must now source another applicant that may or may not be as viable, the HR and MIS departments that had to process all the paperwork to bring that person on board and finally, the remaining staff who have been complaining about being under-staffed and having to pull more than their share has to wait now until another candidate can fill the void. All this because the introduction wasn't set up to succeed. Setting the stage for their arrival and introduction can avoid costly, unnecessary turnover.

Fast-forward now. We have initially integrated them into their unknown surroundings and made them somewhat comfortable with the associates with whom they will be peers. Their training plans have been developed, and the implementation has begun. Good work – job well done. They are starting to show signs of assimilation and have been observed in conversation with their fellow workers. The grace period extended to the new person is varied and often determined by the pending workload. Perhaps there is even a degree of turmoil or unrest created because a backlog has accumulated due to the lack of a complete and cohesive team since the resignation or termination of the one being replaced. If the stress and urgency caused by a failure to observe the buildup and some action to diminish and resolve it by those in the leadership role didn't occur, the worst-case scenario will play out. Failure to act before it becomes a workplace-wide pending explosion is foolhardy, and the disgruntled will be allowed to assume control. If not thwarted, the resulting action will be the throwing to the wolves of the innocent, virginal newbie. When operating shorthanded is the perception of the regulars; the belief is that time, money, and attention are wasted trying to bring them "up to speed" where they can truly become an asset. This can often become as deadly to the new member as any first-day water cooler ogling that might have taken place. It usually leads to a lunch break escape with scorched tire marks in the parking lot. Again, it was a bad ending for all involved. To obtain short-term achievement and long-term prosperity, detailed and proper training is imperative <u>before</u> they can be turned loose to perform independently with little to no supervision. Firsthand experience has revealed to me that the natural inclination of fellow workers is to stick that new person in a role that they believe anyone can perform satisfactorily. The learning curve is a plodding grade, and "even a monkey could do it." The belief is that they will be contributing to the big picture but will be doing so without having their time "wasted" with non-essential training activities and such while the rest of the team busts their collective butts. They don't realize they are setting up their entire operation for potential damage to the end product, reputation for quality, and the relationship with the new coworker. One of the slogans we touted in better days was, "Training doesn't cost...it pays."

Allow me to relate a prime example of the situation I mentioned above. I managed a staff of roughly two dozen at the large printing company I was employed by. As in any industry, we had turnover. Some terminations were beneficial to the operational good, but mostly, those lost were the folks you wished had stayed on once they graduated college and became determined to find their "real" job. Inevitably, you spend your time recruiting, screening, interviewing, and ultimately hiring the person you believe will best possess the desired skill set and, importantly, become part of your existing team. Personalities are as crucial as talents and experience. A non-cohesive group of workers will be much less effective and productive in the short and long terms. The wrong choice of new hire can be the catalyst for unforeseen and undesirable additional turnover. When our company hired a new person and was in the stages of training, others on the team had a propensity to ask that person to break away from their assigned modules or hands-on training involving a certified training associate and "help out" while we were in the throes of a "rush." If the supervisor on shift wasn't paying close enough attention or they were jumping into battle to service the influx of customers, they would often find the newbie "helping out" in the binding area of the production room. What could go wrong? For several reasons, the binding area was one of the first areas introduced to new hires. It was a relatively simple task to be learned and mastered. It was remote from the front of the location and far indeed from customer interaction. It also allowed for a "big picture" view of the entire operation as a team member could bind printed material, keep their head up, and observe all other store areas. Thus, from this vantage point, they can see customer flow, printing production, editing work performed, etc., and feel how it all fits together to run smoothly and efficiently. So, yes, having a new person jump in to "help out" in binding was a no-brainer, as they say, but an error on their part could send the entire remaining team into turmoil. Upon realizing the mis-punch or jamming of the equipment, someone else must then cease their function and respond. Often, this will snowball into others needing

to alter their tasks to either address reprinting what
was just ruined or move to another area vacated by the
teammate who had to respond to the binding area. The
perception of short-handedness can impact both sides
of the counter. Your team feels it as added pressure,
and the customer feels it as underwhelming service
levels.

The key here is for the manager or supervisor to
convince and reassure their teams that they can handle
the workload and will be better in the long run,
allowing that new member to achieve the training
necessary. That mastery will ultimately embody them
with the confidence in themselves and the
determination to demonstrate that they now belong on
your team. It will bring many dividends to that group,
allowing them the time and resources to garner the
required certification. Failure to do so will lead to a
vicious cycle of recruiting, hiring, training, and
termination. Worse still is the potential loss of your
valued employees, who will ultimately tire of this cycle
and the perpetual chaos and eroding product quality it
will bring. Pride in a job well done is, for many, one of
the intangibles that keep them in their current career.
When you take that away with this lack of vision and
consistency, they, too, will become victims of your
mismanagement.

Always Answer The Phone

I've supervised hundreds of team members over the last 40-plus years and never had anyone say I didn't treat them fairly. I've had to terminate the employment of many of those employees, and I'm proud to say that some of them still keep in touch. Many had positive things to say about me in their exit interviews. So many have told me that I was the best boss they ever had. Honest individuals made these comments with nothing to gain by extolling unearned flattery of a manager with whom they were terminating an employment relationship, so I believe them to be sincere. I tried to take the best qualities I learned from my supervisors, managers, and instructors and combine them to develop my management style. Some influencers demonstrated desirable qualities and traits, whereas others exhibited the opposite. Skinner had his box to illustrate the theory of operant conditioning. My interactions with some of my supposed superiors had the same effect on me and the others they supervised.

One of those I floundered under was obsessed with the cleanliness and orderliness of our shared manager's office. On his list of priorities, his office domain was paramount, and all other operational activities were secondary. I watched one day in amazement when he tossed an unemptied waste can out through the office door in a rage. Meanwhile, the entire retail pharmacy he was in charge of was ramshackle and disorganized but relatively unnoticed on his radar and left to those on his management team to address. The team members would approach me with questions and seek direction on their duties as they feared his reprisal. I ensured they were customer-focused and performed cleanliness tasks to keep the place from potential decrepitude and implosion. You might think he was a "big picture" guy, and I was left to handle the mundane daily tasks so he could focus his attention where it was required. That couldn't be further from the truth. The "big picture" is those mundane, daily activities that separate the superior, people-focused, service-focused businesses from those self-interest operations that ultimately collapse upon themselves from within because of grandiose self-indulgent thinking. Shortly after this most recent tirade, I was promoted to general manager at a different location of this national chain. I assigned his observed behavior to the "what not to emulate" file. It's about respect and not asking your team to do a task you wouldn't do yourself. If you wish to have an open-door policy, you had better be approachable to anyone at any time with any issue, suggestion, or question. There cannot be an atmosphere of fear or uncertainty when it comes to the collective beliefs of your team regarding your core values, integrity, and ethics. What they see on the surface must also match what they see behind closed doors.

If there is one legacy I desire to leave in the hearts of those I had working relationships with, it is the confirmation that everyone earnestly believed that when they needed me for something, I was there for them. I always answered my phone. Whether in the middle of the night or while on vacation, I always answered their call for help or advice – no exceptions. So many of these people were precious to me; some were just bodies filling roles in the organization, but my response was always the same. The true reward for me at the end of my career is that they will remember me as someone who was the person with the answer they needed when they needed it. I was the ear when you had to unload it. The muscle when you were moving it. The vault when you needed strict confidence. The cheerleader when you were down or in joining you in congratulations when you were celebrating it. The tour guide when you slipped off the trodden path, and the sounding board when you took a chance and needed moral support. Moreover, I hope that in every case, they remember me as the person who always answered my phone when they called. From the friend with marital problems, the sick teammate that would not be in to work, and often – "the car won't start Boss – what should I do?" calls, not to mention the middle of the night call that an armed robbery had just occurred at work. The incredible degree of terror, panic, and fear coming through the phone line was heart-wrenching. How could I live with myself and show my face to that terrified soul if I had just rolled over and let voicemail pick up the call? When this occurred, our location was open 24 hours every day. For me, the only option was to throw on some clothing, race to the location, reassure the team member that everything would be alright, and get them home to safety immediately after the police finished their investigation. In all cases, I always answered the call. I never let it roll over to voicemail or the answering machine - or in the old days before such gadgets, ignoring it altogether. I believe that you sign an invisible contract with those who look up to you for direction, support, and, in some cases, lifestyle guidance. They are the ones who determine how deep your relationship parameters are. They become part of your extended family and deserve to be treated as such. Everyone dreads that middle-of-the-night phone call, but you must pick up the receiver and dive in headfirst to whatever the situation is. You own it - no excuses. There were innumerable times when my phone would ring while I was in attendance at a sporting event, a church function, one of my children's school functions, or enjoying a meal in a restaurant. Elegant events or watching a movie with the family on my day off, I was always "on call." The inevitable trill of the instrument would be heard, and my wife would give me the evil stare-down because she was aware that I would always answer the call. It certainly wasn't beneficial to our relationship, but I believe it was my obligation and solemn duty to respond each time. I looked at that liability from the opposite side of the coin. If I needed help or the answer to a pressing issue beyond what I could solve or didn't have the authority to respond, I would want my supervisor always to answer their phone and give me the guidance I needed.

Being "on call" 24/7 can become over-taxing to your mental and physical well-being; however, with an empowered and well-trained team, you are usually the last one called because your loyal subordinates will make every attempt to determine a solution and try not to disturb you. These support staff will aid you in innumerable ways throughout your career. You would most likely be amazed at the number of situations that arose and were perfectly resolved without your slightest knowledge. Empowering your team to make those decisions without your approval will save you many phone calls, emails, and text messages. With the true desire to build the very best team, you can train, administer, and encourage your folks to have the tools and resources needed to make critical decisions independently. In that case, you have progressed as a manager from the reactive stage to the proactive stage. Your personal life will benefit greatly. It is much easier to give after-the-fact criticism and "next time" advice to those who went out on a limb and extended their comfort zone to determine the best response and outcome than to remain a hand-holding manager every step of the way. Some managers fear letting go of the decision-making process because they believe it diminishes their role and value to the organization. If you can't let go, you will never be able to grow and promote your team into advanced leadership opportunities. They will either begin to believe that they are unworthy of learning new skills and becoming a playmaker in your operation, or they will become frustrated and bored or move onto a new, more challenging position elsewhere. Again, either way, you lose, as does your organization.

Even the most self-assured, confident assistant must reach out occasionally. When they do ultimately feel they must seek your opinion or approval, you should always ask the caller, when answering the phone, what they believe is the correct solution <u>before</u> doling out any advice. If they are of the caliber that you believe them to be, they will propose similar solutions to those you would have offered with maybe just a few minute details to be adjusted in your collective discussion. By not automatically rattling off the scenario you best believe suits the situation but instead, soliciting their thoughts, you have confirmed to them that they possess the need skills and critical thinking to take them to the next level. The best leaders supply the necessary tools, set a clear focus, assemble a great team, and then get out of the way and let them shine.

So many times, throughout the years, a member of my team at work or someone in my household will mention a problem they face, and without skipping a beat, I automatically offer a solution. This has been a boon in the workplace because it has enabled me to advance through leadership roles and demonstrate the capacity to manage large teams and develop successful organizations. Make no mistake, I am no Solomon, but there have been times when a child, friend, or acquaintance will look at me with what can only be described as amazement at my off-the-cuff responses. This is not always a desirable talent. My wife will attest to my being "controlling" and always offering advice - even when unsolicited. I was approached by a fearless member of my team years ago who stated she was pleased working under me and appreciated how I treated everyone. Still, she had become frustrated because I would make all these split-second decisions and not solicit feedback from the rest of the team before deciding the approach we would take. I had never seen it that way before. My rosy-eyed view was that I was helping them by taking on the tough chore of policy and operational standard setting. In reality, I was stifling their creativity and development to become leaders themselves. That lesson was eye-opening and taken to heart. I learned to approach situations individually and uniquely, driven by consideration for the parties involved and their degree of ownership. If warranted, I just flat-out made decisions, and we collectively moved forward, or I solicited input from a few or many, and we then collectively made the decisions and, again, moved forward.

Now that I have hung up my manager's hat and left the workforce, I wonder about my impact on the lives of those I crossed paths with. I had many notes of congratulations sent to me upon the announcement of my pending retirement, and some were exceptionally sentimental. One stated that I set an example of how to relate to other humans and lead teams. He similarly modeled his behavior and expressed gratitude for knowing me and being part of my family. But the problem that fascinates me the most is what became of employees I had long ago and maybe even only for a short while. I crave the knowledge of where they ended up, how their lives turned out, if they are satisfied with those lives, and most quizzically, whether I impacted those results. I'm nothing special in the grand scheme of the world, of course, and certainly don't see myself as any spiritual influencer. Still, I genuinely desire to be assured that my efforts and interactions were somehow helpful to someone else's humanity. I touched so many lives, and I ask myself the ultimate question – was that chance meeting beneficial to us both, and did I maybe help lead them in a direction that they are now thankful for? I can attest that they have certainly helped in shaping the person I have become. I desire to be remembered by those who reported to me in one fashion or another or were my peers as an honest, loyal, funny, and caring man of integrity. Your word is your bond, and that's all you have in the end. Say what you mean and mean what you say.

Empowerment

I mentioned that a successful leader will empower their team to make decisions. This is undeniably true and cannot be overstressed. Not only can the empowered team make decisions, but they will inherently police themselves and take corrective actions amongst themselves in the areas of discipline and training. I have seen it so many times where a team member is perceived to be pulling less than their fair share of the collective weight, and the other members discuss it amongst themselves and then proceed to confront that team member. The result of that confrontation is most often a resolution of the problem and one in which all interested parties feel a sense of release and almost relief, mainly because they didn't have to "Tell the Boss." The offending worker returns with no shame or blemish on their work record. It's a win-win for all parties.

 Not everyone, however, is comfortable with that "power." Some members of your team are much more inclined to stand behind their manager or supervisor and remain in the background while a conversation with a customer or other teammate occurs. They do not wish to take on the responsibility of ownership and prefer to take direction and not try to affect the status quo. The best methodology for these folks is to allow them to remain in the shadows but involve them in decision-making circles without being aware that they are doing so. You can start small with a simple discussion about what time is best for them to take their lunch break or what color the breakroom should be painted. If they participate in those lesser promptings for an opinion, their confidence can be boosted and future interactions assured by affirming their contribution with praise. "I can't believe how much brighter this room looks painted that color!" If the opportunity arises to offer that praise in the presence of other teammates, the impact is magnified. Next thing you know, they are involved in a conversation about how best to arrange the stockroom, and then they speak up in a customer situation or field an angry phone call. Develop them slowly and gently until they gain confidence and momentum. Some might never get there, but that's okay, too. Every organization needs a delegation hierarchy; some will fall to the bottom. It doesn't mean they are any less vital to success.

For some, empowerment is synonymous with confrontation. One method I always used for myself and tried to impart to others is what I call the "headfirst" approach. The first step is to say what you want to get across in the initial conversation and back it up with additional supporting points in the discussion and the following exchanges. However, the critical element in this approach is to say your objective aloud as the very first remark – "headfirst." Once you have done that, there can be no back-sliding on your part. If instead of stating your desired outcome, you allow for the possibility of alternate reasoning or excuses, you might be tempted to merely take the more straightforward solution that may be offered first by your counterpart. If you rely on allowing the debate to build to your main objective, you may end up walking away feeling empty and somewhat embarrassed or humiliated because the desired resolution is now not likely or possible.

For me, the best possible retail or service experience is when the teammate you encounter possesses the "Yes we can" attitude. There are still a notable number of businesses out there that practice this philosophy and instill it in the members of their respective organizations. The clothing retail giant that I frequent has this mentality. I have never had a dissatisfactory

experience there. Whether I am at the cashier station, wandering the aisles, returning something that didn't fit or just wasn't wanted, the experience is the same. Greeted. Asked if you need assistance. No probing questions were asked during a return interaction. No receipt? No problem. "Can I help you find something?" "Let me call another location to see if they have it in your size." Then, while cupping a hand over the phone, "Yes, they do have it – would you like me to have them hold it for you?" Smile, smile, smile. Unless they change their mantra and alter their service model, I will shop here forever. The teams in their stores have been empowered to make those decisions without having to "call the manager." By entrusting their employees to make on-the-spot decisions, the customer doesn't experience frustration within the transaction. Nor is there the anxious anticipation you dread awaiting the explanation as to why they cannot meet your needs from some random authoritative figurehead within the organization. It shouldn't come to that extreme, and by giving the teams the leeway to make those front-line resolutions, the customer experience is satisfying every time. Having developed teams delegated this autocratic privilege (after adequate training), the result has been richly rewarding. The most significant results were customer satisfaction, individual growth, and much less time and effort required to address customer needs. The conversation with the members of my teams has always included two main points. Primarily, there are very few decisions that they could make that would cause any substantial harm to the overall organization if those decisions met the criteria of:
A.) Leaving the customer pleased and likely to return in the future and
B.) There was no danger to, or blemish of, the company's image due to their actions.
I remind them they always have the option to seek confirmation or counsel before setting a final solution. If they are at a loss of how to proceed, the correct

action is to consult their direct supervisor while keeping the customer involved in the solution. They need to know you are always in the background to back them up. Occasionally, they are flustered, unsure, and just "over their heads." The skilled manager will know instinctively when they should step in and remove the team member from the interaction if they sense they are struggling and uncomfortable.

I relate to a recent experience where my hope for exceptional customer service was rekindled. My wife and I had decided to splurge a little and obtain our dinner meal from a restaurant instead of our usual routine of home cooking and frugality. It was a Friday afternoon, and she had just finished her workday. I had spent my day trying to compose something interesting for my readers and, thus, hadn't made any concrete decisions regarding what I would scramble up for our supper. In this new post-pandemic environment, my wife now enjoys the luxury of working from our home office two days per week, and since her commute time is nil, she and I opted to pick up something prepared by someone else. We are far from extravagant, so we merely ordered from a chain restaurant with a scheduled pick-up time of 20 minutes – just enough time to make the trip to the restaurant. She selected a salad and I a sandwich. We battled a rather fierce rainstorm and ventured out.

As we were navigating our route to the location, she received a confirmation email that our order was ready for pick-up and would be available in the designated location within the restaurant. Upon arrival a few minutes later, we were somewhat perplexed that our food wasn't awaiting us as promised. As there was only one other order on the shelf, we weren't merely overlooking our prepared order; it was simply not there. Within moments, a younger gentleman in uniform of the restaurant chain inquired if we required help. He was identified on his nametag as Josh and held a position as part of the management staff in that location. I explained that we had placed a pre-paid order and received a confirmation email stating that it was ready for pick-up, but it wasn't on the shelf as expected. He gently asked the location we had selected for pick-up, and I informed him we had opted for that particular option. At this point, he revealed that we had mistakenly chosen a location a few miles from where we were. As we had frequented this site in the past and had driven through the area often, I had made the incorrect assumption that this was the location that matched the option listed from the choices given when my wife asked which she should select. Since our prior visit, a new location had opened for business that I wasn't aware of, and I had chosen that one by error, thinking it was our known spot. Although her embarrassment greatly exceeded my own, I was still somewhat flustered and humiliated by my mistake but immediately put at ease by his response. "That happens all the time," he assured us. He then asked what our order was and stated he would have his kitchen team make our meal immediately. He would also phone the other location, explain the circumstances, and instruct them to destroy our original order. As we had already paid for the meal, he refused any additional payment and insisted that we enjoy a soft drink while awaiting our food preparation. Incredible! That is precisely how a practiced manager should respond to such a situation. My wife was more concerned about the loss of profitability of both locations and the possible admonishment of the respective staff. I explained that those repercussions should be the last concern in a case such as this. The goodwill generated from the solution rendered would outweigh any small food cost waste they experienced, and the potential good "word of mouth" could not be bought with any money. Can you train a manager to respond instinctively like this, or is it inherent to their nature? My experience with Josh was genuine, and I believe he relates to people naturally.

Say what you will about Amazon and how they are stifling or thwarting the smaller retailers, but they have never disappointed me. Their product line, speed of delivery, return policy, and processes are far superior to everyone else's. The degree to which their website functionality outshines others is astounding. Laborious layered circles blemish the most well-known retailers' web presence, which you must navigate to hopefully arrive at a desired result if you are fortunate enough to get there. I've encountered many sites where frustration builds to the breaking point, and I dejectedly close the page and move on to a different vendor to satisfy my needs. The staff or team that welcomes me to their establishment, offers assistance without being overbearing or surveilling about it, serves me promptly, and smiles while they are doing it, will always win my undying loyalty. Their genuine "Thank you for your business" departing words will make me return again and again.

Now, let's talk about the exact opposite side of the service coin. What is perhaps the largest electronics retailer in the United States has not seen a dime of my money since 2014 and most likely never will again. It is not because they do not have the largest selection of televisions, computer equipment, gadgets, and all the little accessories sought by today's consumers. Undeniably, they do. It is, instead, because they pissed this customer off so much on my last shopping trip that I vowed never to return, and I have held fast to my pledge since. Now, do not kid yourself that my boycott of their stores will bankrupt them, but if they angered enough customers with their dealings, it could ultimately impact their financial performance. Here's the story that led me down this path of hatred and ire.

In 2014, my wife and I had just purchased new cell
phones. We bought them at our carrier site, which, as
luck would have it, occupied retail space right next
door to this giant retailer. When we were working with
the phone representative, he stated that something was
blocking his ability to transfer our contact information
to the new phones. He advised us to go to his neighbor
and speak with the tech team they have in all their
locations. We did so. The very helpful techie said he
could do it easily but needed his supervisor's
permission to waive the transfer fee. I spoke with the
manager when he came over after a brief wait and
explained the circumstances. He questioned my loyalty
as a customer by searching my purchases in his
system. The roughly five thousand dollars we had
spent in the prior few years on televisions, laptops,
desktops, and tablet computers wasn't enough for him
to waive the twenty-five dollar fee. I would have gladly
paid the cost, but after his lack of appreciation for our
prior business and smugness in the demonstration of
his supposed authority before the team of embarrassed
tech desk employees, I decided I would never darken
the doors of that business again. They often offer items
at substantially lower prices than their competitors, but
I'd pay ten times that amount or do without. As of this
writing, it's been nearly ten years since this experience,
and I am still as angry as I was then. My only hope is
that the "manager" found another career path and isn't
subjecting unfortunate underlings to his horrendous,
pretentious, and self-important strutting.

What You See Is What You Get

In every corporate hierarchy, there exists the "visit" and inspection of the operation performed by the "Big Boss." Sometimes, this review is unannounced and often quite a surprise to those on staff when it occurs, causing anxiety, confusion, and completely forgetting the duties of the moment. The result is usually a scramble to appear as "business as usual" if that, in reality, was an exact representation of the protocols ascribed to by the corporate office. This, of course, is rarely the reality. Most often, these visits are announced in advance, and the date and timetable are well communicated, by upper management, which is most often a local or regional manager position somewhere below the dignitary about to perform the inspection. The unforeseen visitation will most often reveal the operation's true nature: actual staffing levels, legitimate representation of service performance, and overall appearance of the location. Awkward recovery attempts may be made at cleanliness, neatness, staff appearance, and other red flag items. However, a seasoned supervisor will see through those attempts and garner an accurate picture of the realistic daily operation. Most multi-unit businesses have a phone chain that the local managers will immediately utilize to warn their peers of the unexpected visitor heading to inspect their location. Although the manager may not be able to salvage the inspection that just occurred on their site, their sister store may benefit from the advanced warning. Perhaps with the heads-up, they can quickly perform housekeeping duties that will please the superior and give the impression that the district as a whole is performing at acceptable company levels, and perhaps even in excellence. This rarely comes to pass. If the initial impression of the visit is negative, it is tough to outweigh that first impression. Still, it persists and most likely always will.

The unannounced visit presents a truer picture of how that location operates every day. This is exactly what your customers see and experience as well as your team. The planned visit creates a picture of how the location is trying to present an operation performing as company expectations dictate but any scratching beneath the veneer reveals the actual status of operations. The genuine image is often an opposite negative derivative of what should be in existence. The norm is for the local management teams to panic and spend what time they have preparing for the upcoming examination of their operations. This often comes at the expense of service levels and store operations as co-workers are given additional tasks for the announced visits. The sheer irony is that if the manager were operationally sound, they would never need to assign these "additional" tasks (often deep cleaning) as they would be part of the regular ritual of daily operations. They often successfully add some window dressing and lipstick to give the impression that they are current in initiatives and proficient in daily operations. Managers caught in this web of deceitful practices merely ride the wave until they drown in their falsehoods and mismanagement. It's only a matter of time before they are found out by their superiors and peers and are shown the door if the monitoring is accurate.

The employees subjected to this style of panic-driven management will also see through the charade of protecting their boss and ultimately leave their employment or, in some rare cases, present their concerns to the next-level management. This doesn't happen often as there is genuine fear and anxiety of reporting a superior without the comfort and belief that their complaint will be acted upon delicately, confidential, and post haste. I applaud those who do go out on a shaky limb for the betterment of themselves, their peers, and the organization. In your management career, you will also encounter an employee who will "cry wolf" and believes your every intention is designed solely for their demise and misery and threatens to file a complaint or may do so. Still, they are few and very far between. They will also either change their tactics and become part of your team if you are an ethical and worthy supervisor or depart from your employ quickly. They present a challenge, and your ability to overcome their attitude will be tested. Still, ultimate success in molding them into a "team player" will further strengthen your skill set and be rewarding.

Whether you direct others in a retail place of business or some service industry, the proper standard of achievement is an operation where physical appearance and customer service are the same every day and not different depending upon circumstance. There must not be a distinguishable difference in the level of genuineness of your team while interacting with clients. They must always immediately greet and interact with the customer if trained and engaged appropriately. Happy, smiling people at every turn. Every day. Every time. Nothing else will suffice. You are answering the phone within three rings – every time. Clean windows, floors, restrooms (whether open to your guests or not), and a sense of orderliness and purpose. Breakrooms must be tidy, and team member ownership of their upkeep is essential to avoid disarray. It must never become a home for dirty, wayward dishes and overflowing trash receptacles.

The same principles are vital for stockrooms and offices. Your team will follow your lead if you exude an air of perpetual orderliness and structure. If it's important to you that the guests are our primary mission in our business, then they will be afforded that same designation by your staff. If you stoop to pick up a small piece of paper on the floor, they will pick up the scrapes they see. If you wash your dishes, they will do likewise. If you walk by a client without engaging them, they will also be ignored by the team member behind the counter. You must always set the example you wish them to emulate. No gesture can be considered too small for consideration. If they observe you texting on your phone in an apparent non-business situation, how can you expect them not to be tempted to pull out their phone and engage in texting or web surfing? Staying at your desk in your office is unacceptable if you genuinely want to be in touch with your team and the reality of how your business operates at any given moment. A friend used to refer to it as M.B.W.A. – Management By Walking Around. The travel path I mentioned earlier is a critical part of this idea. Walking the building's perimeter inside and out, along with the many facets inside, including restrooms, sales floor, dining area, and production floor frequently on any given day, will automatically build your "To Do" list.

What's important to you will become your priorities for the immediate future and will be proactive steps to be addressed long before your customer base might have noticed them. The beauty of this is often two-fold. First, you are never operating from a fireman's perspective, overwhelmed by the "fires" and catastrophes piling one atop another that you must now "put out." The second benefit is that your teams will pick up on those critical items you have brought to their attention for resolution often enough. In contrast, now, they notice and correct them before you ever observe them! With this self-awareness, your team is always at its peak. Any corporate visitation, whether announced or unannounced, will, upon inspection, reveal that your operation is always the same, and there is no panic or dread of those occasions. Your teams will not stress themselves much more than on any typical day and will often have the opportunity to bask in the limelight bestowed by the visiting dignitary. As a successful and confident leader, you should never experience the apprehension of an interaction between a member of your team and any corporate official. Instead, you can proudly lead the exchange and allow your employee to shine and be recognized for their efforts and dedication. So many managers are afraid to relinquish the spotlight, but I can guarantee that they will never let you down when you hold your players up.

My personal experience with these visits has most often been pleasant and of the second variety, where we stressed much less than our peer locations. Quite frequently, the style of supervisor you report to will dictate your experience. I have had the opportunity to report to multiple district or multi-unit managers, and the experience has been primarily enjoyable and a few times contemptible. The determining factor in those interactions was how my immediate supervisor addressed any criticisms forthcoming from their next-level or higher boss. The lesson I gleaned from those events was this. Protect your teams from upper management. If the visiting director observes a deficiency, the district manager has two options. They can either take the criticism as their deficiency and own it, acknowledging they are responsible for their team, or they can deflect responsibility to their manager, who now sits on the hot seat. The latter will turn on you, inquire about or criticize your performance, and demand an explanation and "action plan." The sole purpose of this behavior is to avoid a lessening of their self-worth in the eyes of their superior and instead appear as the person who will address this calamity and rectify it by whatever means necessary. Most often, you come off looking incompetent and embarrassed, all for the sake of their self-esteem and job security. You walk away with a painful back from being thrown under the bus and sporting a new set of knife wounds. My personal experience is that the relationship with your supervisor is forever damaged in the aftermath of such a visit. No trust now exists between you and most likely, never can again.

I had such an experience once with a district manager for the pharmacy chain I was employed with. Upon an inspection, the regional manager questioned the placement of a new item recently cut into a vitamin planogram. The directive was that the store brand was always facing to the right of the name brand, but for this particular item, it was specified to place it to the left, and I had done so. When questioned, Pete turned on me like a rabid dog and demanded an explanation. I prided myself on my performance and following directives and stated that it was explicitly instructed to be placed there. He insisted that I show them the directive. I retrieved it from the office and, feeling somewhat angry and frustrated, showed the corporate memo to them. Pete mumbled something to the effect of "Well, how do you like that?" and resumed the inspection without apologizing or acknowledging his childlike behavior and arrogance. The remainder of the visit went fine, and fortunately, Pete was transferred shortly after that. Being the worst example of this management style, he was replaced by perhaps the best example of how to treat your people. Craig immediately established himself as respectable, honest, and the polar opposite of the maniacal Pete. He quickly learned who his "go-to" managers were and set up his hierarchy and network of responsibility. If you were dependable enough to perform as expected and directed and had a history of absolute steadfastness, you were asked to take on more responsibility and help lead the bigger team. If there was ever an occasion where your performance was called into question by higher echelon or you were considered for advancement, Craig was your champion. He would take any criticism as exclusively his own and, if necessary, have a future conversation with you privately to address any area of concern. He was a back-slapper and a genuine pleasure to be around. Sometimes, that boss/employee line is tricky and oftentimes leaders are hesitant and uneasy about being an actual friend but not with him. We even shared season tickets for the NFL team in our city, and our relationship lasted beyond our mutual employment. With that being said, however, you still knew the line existed in the workplace and that it could never be crossed in an unethical business manner.

When I assumed the role of multi-unit manager, I modeled my behavior as an aggregate of the behaviors and examples of those I had experienced during my prior employment positions. From lowly stockboy at a paint and wallpaper store to crew supervisor to assistant manager to manager of the highest-grossing regional location of a national chain or manager of an international print giant, the lessons learned continually influenced my behaviors and beliefs. I graduated from university with a degree in history and certification to teach social studies, and yet here I was, following a path unforeseen to me while in school. Something about leading others and bringing about a needed service appealed to me, and I ended up with a gratifying career. As a leader and sometimes trainer, I have been able to adapt and use the teaching skills I gained studying education in college. With every group I've encountered along the way, I have learned as much from them as they have from me, but the best lessons were gained while attending "Sidewalk University." Life is truly the best teacher. If you take a bird's eye view of any situation, there are truisms for the attentive.

Take A Chance On Them

There often are moments when you can break from the accepted norm, take a detour, and become a better human being because of it. When holding a position in which you make hiring decisions, you have that choice quite often, and often, you can make a decision that can affect someone's entire future for the better. Now and again, an applicant will come across your desk or walk in your front door, someone whom you may never have considered hiring before, and thus, present you with a prospect that may never have crossed your mind previously. Selecting a candidate dramatically different from the ideal individual can be uncertain and frightening, but the rewards can be vast.

One such opportunity presented itself to me relatively early on in my career when I was approached by an agent of an organization that specialized in the placement of disabled and under-represented individuals who had either experienced a debilitating injury or had difficulties in mobility or communication. After meeting with this representative, I agreed to meet some of the candidates represented by the agency. Their distinct personalities and incredible attitudes immediately enamored me. One amazing woman had been in a terrible automobile accident a few years prior. She had sustained a traumatic brain injury that left her wheelchair-bound and unable to use one arm. Additionally, her speech patterns were slowed and sometimes broken by moments of forgotten words or the inability to completely express her thoughts in the expected time assumed by the listener. She would require bus transportation to attend the workplace and some additional modification of the production area but otherwise was agreeable to the requirements of any potential employment. Although I had other, more traditional candidates available for the currently posted position, I contacted our HR department for counsel and advice. I decided to hire and bring her on board. There were growing pains and some uncertainty in the early stages of her training and assimilation into our business model. Still, after a concise timeframe, the team became enamored with her, as did our customer base. What may have been uncertain, delicate interactions with teammates and clients soon became everyday banter and camaraderie. She quickly became a regular team member and wasn't perceived differently than anyone else. She was expected to perform the duties she was hired for and did so in a more than adequate way. I continued to align with that organization and employ others with similar circumstances. I was never disappointed in hiring those who may have been otherwise overlooked in the job market.

I consider myself to be a very personable person. I have had recruiting and hiring responsibilities in every position since high school. I have learned that you truly get a much more precise, more faithful picture of your applicant by making them comfortable in the interviewing environment and asking questions not pre-scripted by the human resources department designed to reveal skills and potential behavior problems. Once their defenses are brought down by casual conversation and they feel comfortable and non-threatened, they, too, will forget their pre-rehearsed answers to the questions they assume you will be asking. Of course, there are so many questions you are forbidden to ask by laws governing employment opportunities. All your HR training is vital because of potential discrimination or bias accusations, and I agree wholeheartedly that they should be avoided and left unasked. Truthfully, they are irrelevant to the hiring decision anyway. When your applicant feels that they can trust you, they are likelier to be honest and tell you everything you need to know about their work beliefs, attitudes, and how well they will fit into your organization. I don't condone trickery or misleading the applicant by any stretch of the imagination. Still, I firmly believe a relaxed conversation will allow you to choose candidates from the pool you have sourced. Canned answers tell you next to nothing about how they will perform once hired. You must seek a clear image of the fires within when presented with the haze of the smoke screen.

A polar opposite hiring decision that demonstrates the need to look outside the traditional applicant box was employing a convicted felon that no one else would consider. Unlike the unanimous acceptability of hiring the sweet, under-appreciated, disabled employee, a need for a different variety presented itself one day, and the decision to hire became much more spiritual and self-reflective for me. This applicant walked into the location and asked to speak to the manager. I was summoned and met the gentleman in the lobby and asked him how I could be of service. He inquired about the entry-level position I had open and whether he could submit an application and be considered. I immediately recognized that he was impeccable in speech and appearance and of obvious intelligence, not to mention older than myself. I asked a few probing questions and determined that he would be an ideal candidate for my business but at a much higher level than the current opening he was inquiring about. I invited him to complete the paper application (pre-online submission), and we would talk once he returned it. I learned early on never to allow what you believe to be a potential exceptional hiring prospect to depart your location before you can at least pre-determine their capabilities and make an appointment for follow-up if agreeable. When possible, an immediate interview is practical and indeed desirable to prevent the next business from hiring them before you can act. Upon

completing his paperwork, I invited him into my office
for a formal interview. I began by reiterating the
nature of the position, the pay rate associated with that
entry-level, and whether he would still be interested in
that offer. I fully anticipated that he would respond
that he hadn't realized the wage level, thank me, and
depart. What transpired then was somewhat life-
changing for me.

His response was direct and genuine. He acknowledged
that the pay rate was substantially less than what he
was accustomed to earning, but he was willing to start
at that level because he brought a troubled set of
circumstances with him in his search for employment.
He further went on to explain that he had recently been
released from prison after serving a multi-year term for
a crime that he was both ashamed of and incredibly
remorseful for perpetrating. He stated that he had been
a successful attorney for many years and had allowed
temptation to overrule good sense in dealing with the
investment finances of some of his clients. He
embezzled money from several of them, and upon
discovering the crime, he was disbarred and convicted.
Newly released from prison, he attempted to get his
feet back on the ground and support his family while
regaining a small portion of his self-esteem and
reputation. He had been rejected, however, at every
turn and faced restitution requirements imposed as
part of his punishment. He had remarried just before
his conviction and incarceration and had fathered a son
with his second wife. The responsibilities of a family
provider and the addition of a newborn presented
desperation he had never experienced. He was a
defeated but proud man who had little left and was
now additionally strapped even tighter by the needs of
a baby. With no potential lucrative opportunity, he was
making the rounds and applying for nearly anything
available to jump-start a new lease on life. Many
businesses precluded him from applying because of

their internal policies regarding prior criminal convictions. He realized he was limited in potential opportunities and was willing to accept a lower starting wage. He spoke candidly about his past and the error he had committed without my prompting. I sat back and listened to his description of life in prison, how his family and friends were negatively impacted by his actions, and how he so despairingly desired to try to make things right for everyone, especially his families – both original and newly acquired. He had children from his first marriage, and their relationships had suffered and been strained from his incarceration. He was in debt to his first wife for alimony and child-support payments missed. Life-long friends would not even return his phone calls. His world had crashed, and he was searching for the shovel to dig himself out. He placed the blame for his troubles entirely and squarely upon his shoulders.

When the interview was complete, I was forever changed, and I offered him the position. Before meeting him, I would have been amongst that group of employers who had passed immediate judgment upon him without meeting him because of his crime. I would have believed that he deserved exactly what he got and couldn't be trusted or relied upon to be part of my organization. My thoughts most likely would have been, "Well, jailbird, what did you expect after what you did?" Thankfully, my hardened heart softened somewhat that day, and I took a chance on him. I firmly believed that I would get some incredible effort and exemplary output from him because of the intelligence and personal skills he brought to the table. I further thought that the first offer for employment elsewhere with a substantially greater rate of income would find him submitting his two-week notice and moving on. I was correct on the first set of assumptions, but I was entirely incorrect regarding his loyalty and tenure. He remained on my team for quite a career, and I later

determined that he had been offered other positions
with other employers throughout his time with me.
However, he remained loyal to me because I had given
him a chance when no one else would. As positions
opened up in my staff for a supervisor and later an
assistant manager, he was promoted several times as a
"no-brainer" perfect candidate for them. The day did
arrive when he gave his notice and moved on. No one in
their right mind would deny that the circumstances of
that resignation were justified. He was smitten with the
Caribbean and had vacationed there many times while
enjoying his career as a successful attorney. He had
told me on many occasions that when he retired for
good, he would love to manage a hotel in St. Maarten,
but he realized it was now a pipe dream. Well,
sometimes dreams do come true. He won the million-
dollar lottery one day on a scratch-off ticket, bought a
hotel on the island, and officially retired. He offered
free room and board to me anytime I wished to come
down and vacation there myself as a "thank you" for
taking a chance and hiring him.

I'm also reminded of a sad tale of a young lady
recommended for hire by one of my team members at
the time. She was painfully shy and had a troubled
past. She had been adopted into a family at an early age
after her parents had abandoned her. She struggled to
feel wanted and loved by the members of her new
"family" and friends of theirs, fellow schoolchildren
she encountered in her new environment, and others.
As she aged into her teens, she had, like so many
others, turned to drugs and self-mutilation. She was
hospitalized several times and in rehab twice as well.
One day, she accompanied that same staffer when he
stopped at work to pick up something he had forgotten,
and I was introduced. I was unaware of her story before
this meeting, so I brought no preconceived notions or
prejudices. I found her very pleasant, albeit somewhat

shy and inward-drawn. At some point during the following months, an opening occurred, and I was asked about her joining our team.

I arranged for an official interview and believed our training team could bring her out of her shyness enough to make her comfortable interacting with clients and fellow teammates. Before I made the decision, the employee making the recommendation filled me in on her history. This presented a small wrinkle in the decision as I had to weigh the likelihood that she might be overwhelmed by the pressures of the position and buckle under the desire to backslide into a return to drug use. The company policy was clear about usage and employment, including a drug test before hire. Under normal circumstances, I would review the policy with a prospective candidate and allow them to self-withdraw if they believed they would be unlikely to pass such a test. It happens more often than most would guess. I've had candidates fail and express surprise that they were detected – not that they didn't pass. In this instance, I presented the employment offer and the precondition testing requirement to her and allowed her to decide. I extended her the employment offer for several reasons. The primary reason is my experience with internal hiring recommendations. Not many employees will recommend a potential candidate if they have any reservations regarding that person's abilities and likelihood of success. They perceive any potential downfall of the applicant as a reflection of their self-worth and importance to the group. They would usually do anything to prevent any negativity from themselves. The other reason was the simple human desire to help this struggling teenager feel normalized and part of something bigger than her troubled past. Maybe she was becoming immersed in employment and involved enough to take what she perceived as the spotlight off of herself, if only long enough to build self-confidence and trust in something.

I, too, was a parent, and I hope someone will do the same for my child.

This story, however, did not have the traditional happy ending. She acclimated to our operation quickly, successfully learned the best methods and operational strategies, and was deemed a successful hire. She continued to grow and integrate into the team for roughly eighteen months, and then suddenly, one day, literally disappeared. Once she was a no-call, no-show for the prescribed three days, I reluctantly terminated her employment per company protocol and policy. I was handcuffed by procedure while saddened and anxious as to her whereabouts. All contacts she had listed, including our team member who introduced her, were unaware of her location and the reasons for her sudden and unannounced departure. It wasn't until a few weeks later that I found out that she had indeed succumbed to the evils of the drug culture and had ended up estranged from her adopted family and everyone else. She sent me a letter of explanation and apology (which I still have) stating that she had indeed slipped back into the darkness of drugs and was hoping to take advantage of what she perceived as her "last chance" with another stint in rehab. I never heard from her again and am very prayerful that, indeed, she did succeed in overcoming this addiction and today lives a beautiful life. Sometimes, the chances you take may not have a fairytale ending, but they are worth it. There are so many lovely stories out there just waiting to be written; all that is needed to begin their tale is for someone to take a chance on them.

One final example highlights a course of action available to leaders that might not be quite obvious. I had recently assumed the leadership of a location in a new state after accepting a transfer within the organization. Having just moved to an area where all landmarks, business relationships, and staffing were completely unfamiliar, I needed to quickly learn who my best players were and how best to organize them for my greatest likelihood of success. It was a dramatic change. Several branches were under my direct control in addition to this "hub" site. It didn't take very long to determine where the strengths and weaknesses were, and the cast of potential future leaders made themselves evident as well. One such rising star was a younger shift leader who had the potential to become a higher-level manager with the proper training and development. This would also require a good deal of coaxing and reaffirmation of her skill set, as she exhibited very little self-assurance or confidence in her own abilities. I knew I would need to encourage and develop her, but the efforts would be so worthwhile as the potential was tremendous. And so, we began. With approval from my boss, I created a specialized classroom training program. I held monthly sessions for all high-potential team members and existing assistant managers to impart additional knowledge omitted by the branded corporate instruction that was offered. I mentioned this in another chapter, but there are types of knowledge you are unaware you do not possess unless it is pointed out to you. These little tidbits of information can be vital to a leader's development. Thus, I enrolled her in this group; as expected, she performed admirably. Before long, she was promoted to assistant manager in the hub location – reporting directly to me. She had recently experienced a divorce and was now a single mother with one child, and she was very much the breadwinner.

One morning, she failed to show up for her shift, and there was general head-scratching and puzzlement as it was utterly uncharacteristic, to say the least, and the fact that there had been no phone call to explain the absence made it even more puzzling. Fast-forward a few days, she has returned to work with an excuse and apology for her absence; all is forgotten, forgiven, and returned to normalcy. She was promoted within a year to a store manager position and had a rewarding career with the company for many years. What she never knew was that I had been made aware that the reason for her absence that day was that she was sitting in a jail cell after being arrested for drunk driving. She had been at a party and had been trying to drown her recent sorrows if just for one evening and allowed it to get out of hand. She was terrified of telling me the truth because she was afraid she would lose her employment and, worse still, lose my respect for her as an employee and, more importantly, as a person. Another trusted employee and the local police had given me the information. I had to decide if I wanted to reside on the side of policy or the side of humanity. I chose the direction that my internal consciousness led me to. Had I reported the infraction to my immediate supervisor, I may have been forced to terminate her employment in the name of corporate righteousness and adherence to cookie-cutter-style practices. The result would have driven a hard-working, incredibly talented, future profitable leader onto the unemployment line. Losing someone with her talents would have been regretful and foolish. I overlooked that misstep and pursued the greater good for all parties involved. I could not fathom jeopardizing her future as a valuable employee to us or elsewhere nor perhaps as a mother with a damaged reputation within the work environment and possibly her social circle. I never mentioned a word of it to her or anyone else, and in my opinion, it allowed a fantastic flower to grow and thrive instead of seeing it as a weed and cutting it out of the garden.

As a leader, you sometimes hold someone's future in your hands and must be able to analyze and weigh the choices and decisions you make daily. This is probably the most significant responsibility of the role you serve.

My teams have consisted of females, males, transgender, straight, gay, multicultural, young, and elderly individuals. Some have been quick to learn and advance; some have encountered challenges and moved on. Some have been very happy in the roles in which they were initially brought on board, and some have left for "greener pastures" only to return. The critical aspect is that while they were with us, they were a welcome part of the team. We didn't bring the outside social issues into our workplace unless extreme forces made it impossible to ignore the preverbal "elephant in the room." Experiences such as September 11th, Rodney King, the financial crash of 08, the COVID-19 pandemic, and George Floyd could not be ignored, and we engaged in honest dialogue to help one another through those delicate and challenging issues. Unity, diversity, honesty, and integrity are the required touchstones of making a team cohesive and inclusive. If you desire to be a successful leader of people, you must possess and practice these qualities. If you aren't sincere, your team will see through the veil of the imposter you present and never adhere to the vision you purport to instill in them.

Additionally, you must weed out any cancerous malignancy brought into your team by members who do not follow this openly supportive framework. If not, they will work to undermine the cohesiveness of your team, create factions and divisions within, and ultimately cause great harm. They often act purely from their own limited mindsets, preconceived notions, stereotypes, irrational jealousies, or suspected favoritism. As Barney Fife strongly advises, "nip it in the bud!"

Be Present In The Moment

So often in today's workplace, there are an enormous number of distractions from various sources that invade every facet of the operation. The manager is forced to address each that comes their way to maintain control and adherence to that day's schedule and plan of action. Phone calls, text messages, emails, conference calls, unannounced visitors, and concerns surfaced by the staff are just a few of these time-wasters. The best and most well-thought-out methods to avoid these trappings will only aid in your sanity occasionally. They cannot be avoided altogether, and you find yourself on the frustrated end of the interruption, often wishing for a way out or a reason to disconnect from the conversation or visit so you can return to your true purpose in monitoring the current activities. When there is no escape for you, and you are hooked into that situation, the worst mistake you can make is allowing it to take exclusivity of your focus. They cannot be allowed to distract your attention from an active interaction (in progress) with your team member or a customer.

Who among us can remember a time when we weren't merely listened to halfheartedly while the person involved in a conversation with us was distracted by an incoming email or text? How about when you were showing or discussing something deemed by you to be an essential item, and the person you were showing it to was instead giving attention to an object in their peripheral vision? It happens often and can be highly frustrating, demoralizing, and usually embarrassing. Imagine attending a baseball game with a good friend, and while detailing an event important to you, they are paying attention to the whereabouts of the hot dog vendor or the cute couple on the "kiss cam." Maybe you are explaining to your spouse why you are late getting home from work. Your minor fender-bender gets little attention because the local news broadcast on the television is announcing the lottery numbers, and they check their tickets. Maybe they turn to you afterward and ask you to repeat what you were saying, or perhaps they fail to see the importance of what you are trying to convey because they never heard the extent of your comment or the tone in which you relayed it. You are often left with little or no desire to repeat yourself and move on to another topic or walk away. Ever ask your child about schoolwork while they are playing video games? Been there and done that?

The very same situations occur within your place of business or office. As the leader, you ought to eliminate the potential for such occurrences. Every team member deserves respect and acknowledgment of your undivided attention while interacting with them. Regardless of who initiates the conversation, you must put your cell phone aside, get up from your computer screen, cease stocking and organizing, cease walking through the area where they reside, or whatever else might divert your attention and engage them directly. Under no circumstance should your team members ever experience the feeling of being "blown off" by you because you allowed another distraction to shake your concentration and break the conversational bond. When your attention is allowed to waver, you insult the other parties involved. This often results in a lessening of their self-worth in their own eyes and a likelihood of future withdrawal from suggestions or conversations that would have created a stronger bond between manager and employee. They may leave the interaction believing you have little or no interest in their thoughts, opinions, or personal life. Damage such as this is tricky to remedy and often leads to turnover.

The introduction of the smartphone has compounded this disturbing practice, which is becoming increasingly prevalent in society and the workplace. Who hasn't witnessed the table of acquaintances at a restaurant where all parties are intently engaged with their devices and completely ignoring one another sitting within arm's reach? It is disheartening and tell-tale of where we are headed as a society. People wandering along a sidewalk, absorbed in their devices, nearly fall off curbs, jostle other walkers, or perhaps step in front of a moving vehicle. With the introduction of cell phones in the hands of managers, we could now stay in touch with our places of business and our teams at all hours of the day or night. That allowed us to never miss a beat as to what was occurring when we were absent from the production floor or retail space—we now had the opportunities to improve our productivity and the ability to monitor endlessly with this tool. Nothing could be more accurate. As a manager, you are now expected always to be connected. Evenings, weekends, and vacations no longer meant you lost touch with the crews at the factory or workshop. Instead, the little taskmaster in your pocket had the potential to vibrate or ring with a request for your attention. In its original incarnation, the phone would require you to physically "answer" it to determine the need on the other end.

As that same device progressed and grew "smarter," the potential for interruption increased exponentially with the addition of texting and email capabilities. Most text messages were a direct result of a known contact's attempt to reach you. These inquiries were so much easier to address than an actual telephone call if they were simple. A more complicated text might require a return phone call to the originator if your response is too complex and possibly misunderstood to address via text message. Email capabilities, however, opened up the receiver to become inundated with known and unknown (spam) emails. The known senders weren't as urgent and could usually be responded to with a more detailed, thought-out response at a later hour. The worst of these emails was the multi-recipient variety in which there were always a handful of unskilled or careless recipients foolish enough to use the "reply-all" key. Talk about your time wasters! Even more recipients on the chain adding to the mess with reply-all responses of "please do not reply-all!"

I return to my topic now. This device has become the leading distractor to genuine direct communication in the modern-day environment, including the workplace. During an average day, the manager is inundated with calls, text messages, and emails on that little overlord czar and must have a method to prevent these vibrating demons from assuming control of every situation and interaction. When approached by your fellow teammate, it's imperative that you not allow yourself to stray from direct eye contact and sincere attention when that monster of disruption sends its tentacles toward your consciousness. Stay on the course and engage fully with your partner until natural fruition is achieved. I encourage you to instruct your teams of your intent to ignore any interruptions that occur while you are engaging with them and that your expectations of them will be the same. Insist that they ignore their smartphones while conversing with their co-workers, including interactions with yourself. The best practice is for their phones to be stowed in lockers or unused while on the production floor, interacting with customers, or on any assignment requiring constant attention. Treat your teams in the same manner you would ask to be treated. If you have ever experienced a supervisor whose attention was distracted by external disturbance, recall how you perceived the snub proffered and vow not to perpetuate that offense upon your audience.

Diverting your eyes from theirs, glancing down at the screen of your smartphone to determine who or what seeks your attention, turning to listen to what another is stating while being spoken to, or walking as your speaker attempts to keep your attention while following your movement are all sins of this covenant. None of these, however, is as disrespectful and demeaning as accepting an incoming phone call and walking away from your engagement in the original conversation to respond to the new caller. I cannot overemphasize its importance. This equates with the proverbial slap in the face. You will lose any merit in the eyes of the person left hanging. I understand that there are calls a leader must accept when they are received—urgent calls from another manager, maybe something personal at home or your immediate superior. Before engaging the incoming caller, you must apologize, explain, and excuse yourself. In most situations such as this, the interruption is forgivable, especially if respect is granted to the other using an explanation for the unforeseen interruption and rudeness.

Suppose your team member engages you in conversation and is regaling you with the details of an event or circumstance. In that case, they deem it necessary enough themselves to relay it to you. If it's considered a "big deal" to them, you should receive and encourage it as an important occurrence or occasion. If you undervalue the importance and significance of their newsworthy item, then you will undermine their perceived self-importance and relationship with you. They may very well "clam up" regarding any future instances that they would like to relate, and any chance to build that rapport that should exist between supervisor and their teams may be lost. If you are being made aware of these events second hand then you have already established a relationship where there is no comfort in dialog from the bottom up and you will not be as close to the team as you might perceive yourself to be. Follow up with them shortly after that to see if there have been any additional developments, and affirm that you are genuinely concerned about their lives outside the office. Be conscious of their desire to broadcast the information to others or keep it confidential and honor their request. Gossip is inappropriate in the office, workplace, or wherever you interact with and build teams. Nothing can be more destructive to the morale and cohesiveness of any organization than uncontrolled gossip and water-cooler talk. Most topics discussed are untrue, unfounded, born out of jealousy, and intended to make the spreader believe they are increasing their self-importance. The poor soul at the butt of the destructive insinuations, rumor, gossip, and scuttlebutt or whispering will lose their belief in the fellowship of the team and may very likely resign from their post. Saying you're sorry after the fact will not mend any fences nor give the maligned individual the desire to return to the team. The proactive and deliberate leader will set the ground rules for the team, address the strict code of conduct forbidding idle gossip, and establish consequences for such malicious behavior.

There is a secondary caution to this topic that I will address in this chapter as well. Although it is less blatant than the acts of rudeness I've mentioned here, the practice of delay or failure to respond to an inquiry sent via text message or email can be hurtful or frustrating to the sender. Most of us have become so attached to our smartphones that we respond to a text message with almost instantaneous speed. The response to email for those who can program their devices to receive incoming messages can be nearly as fast. If the sender of a message is aware of our habits regarding the frequency of checking our phones and response speed to incoming messages, then delay or neglect on our part when they transmit a notification of some inquiry or notification can become an offense to them. The lack of response or delay in the reply is greatly exacerbated upon the determination that we have reacted to others who have been sent while ignoring theirs. Under normal circumstances, one would think this somewhat absurd and impossible knowledge, but I ask you to consider this relatively new complication. If they are in contact with us because of a workplace connection or on a personal level, they most likely have additional means of contact or connection. Suppose they are "friends" or "following" on Facebook, Twitter, Instagram etc., or have observed you texting others or merely interacting with your device. In that case, they know you have seen their offering and CHOSEN not to respond or prioritize them to the bottom of the attention hierarchy. When there is no response from you, what else can the offended party believe? The slight most likely is unintentional, but the damage can be severe.

Praise Over Pizza

Hey! Who doesn't like a free lunch? I, for one, will always accept an invitation to eat on someone else's dime. My appetite seems more prominent when the boss is footing the bill. I've enjoyed so very many celebratory luncheons, dinners, breakroom parties, and alcohol-fueled binges that it's miraculous I don't weigh more than I do. I've sponsored just as many within my career and for various teams. As a manager, the ability to bring a reprieve into the workplace and lessen the tension or reward the exceptional effort of the staff during an unusually stressful situation with food or drink is a time-proven tool in your arsenal. The number of pizzas delivered to my places of business would make any Italian proud, and the number of cold cuts dished up with potato salad and chips could weigh down a large delivery van. Without fail, the teams respond to such goodie-fests. They will appreciate the moments when they can remove themselves from the usual activities or craziness currently at hand and relax with some tasty treat. Hopefully, several team members can take a break at the exact moment to also engage in fellowship and small talk to lessen the moment's stress. A better solution is to hold this soiree during off hours, so the tension is substantially less and somewhat of a party atmosphere can exist. A relaxed, celebratory ambiance can erase many workplace catastrophes and turn tension into an enjoyable event.

These small reward-inspired offerings are lovely for morale and cost-effective for the organization, or the manager should the expense not be covered by company discretionary funds. They can be applied at short notice and often as an off-the-cuff response to an unforeseen or business event. The card can be dealt at any time and will most likely please most of your team.

You will have coworkers who will naturally complain about where the pizza or food item is ordered from, the timing of the surprise feast, the amount of effort exerted by others on the team, and how much or little they deserve to participate in the reward. It would help if you did not allow these naysayers or wet blankets to tarnish the intent of your actions. I recall a staffer who approached me after one of these pizza splurges and complained that because he worked a later shift, I should have the courtesy to phone him before he departed for the office and alert him regarding my intent to purchase food to be shared amongst the team so he would know not to pack and bring his lunch that day. Can you believe it? I'm sure the managers and supervisors reading this will be shaking their heads in the affirmative because we all have employed personalities similar to this. I smile about this memory now in retirement but can easily recall my internal anger after his rebuke and vowed never to order food when he was scheduled on that day. After a short respite, I forgot my bitterness and resumed the occasional workday or offsite function. However, I never entertained the notion of making that forewarning phone call to him.

Pizza and the like are excellent little rewards for a quick morale boost and will likely keep your teams happier than they would be without them. Still, for many folks, a word of thanks, praise, or general appreciation will go much farther in keeping them engaged in the team collective. Taking someone aside and expressing gratitude or admiration for a job well done will elevate their self-worth and investment in the long-term goals and vision of the organization much more than any monetary or stomach-pleasing award. The only action with a more significant impact is to proclaim those same statements of praise in the presence of the remainder of their peers. By making this announcement, you are elevating them to a higher tier in the eyes of their fellow workmates. Every successful manager has an instinct regarding hidden talents possessed by their staffers, and by gentle manipulation of their psyches, these attributes can be nudged forward into the light. When developing future leaders, giving public praise has the compound effect of allowing them to believe in their own skill set and reinforcing their value to the others they will someday lead. If you are relying upon them to perform as well or better than they did at this event, a public extolling before the group will ensure they will respond in the future with as much zeal as on this day, if not more so because they will seek additional praise and perform in the desired manner to ensure that you award them with the same enthusiasm. I am not condoning using this tactic to manipulate team members into performing beyond their expected roles with the expectation of future rewards that you would not intend to award. Dangling a carrot is only ethical when the horse has a realistic chance of eating it and not chasing the ever-elusive feed bag. Moral behavior is paramount to attaining successful managerial longevity. Employing the "bait and switch" may return a short-term objective, but in the long run, your teams will discover your proper disposition and abandon you.

Managing teams requires that you have a pulse on the morale and well-being of your associates and the ability to find a diversion to address any lessening of the overall mental health and stability. I am reminded of an episode that will yield an example of the myriad possibilities available to break the monotony of the daily grind. This example will highlight another point I wish to address in this chapter. In the mid-nineties, I managed a team of roughly twenty employees in a multi-unit international printing company. When the location opened a few years prior, I was hired to set up the operation and I had assembled this team. Building my team from the ground up without inheriting those already in place from the prior management team, as I had experienced in previous positions I held, was so refreshing. I carefully selected those I believed would allow us to hit the ground running once we were open for business and fully operating. I made some needed changes and additional hires in those first years but was very pleased with the assembled crew overall.

The summertime was beginning, and traditionally, our business slowed down somewhat; production would sometimes sag, and general boredom would occasionally set in. I would assign special projects and do in-depth cleaning of the location and equipment to keep idle hands busy, but any diversion to the redundancy would be greatly appreciated. I had no intention of layoffs or other labor-reducing necessities unless absolutely unavoidable. In fact, many on the team would take a vacation or personal time to lessen the overstaffing.

One day, while listening to the local radio station as I drove to the office, I heard of a contest they were sponsoring, and I immediately gave it my full attention. They were awarding an all-expenses paid event at a local theme park that was a favorite of nearly every thrill seeker and beachgoer in the area. To enter the contest, a representative of the company or office was required to submit a letter stating who they were, what they did as a business, and why they believed they were the best choice for deserving this prize. I considered our chances of winning the contest as an extreme longshot, to say the least, but sat at my desk and composed what I believed was a clever letter explaining our business, our team of deserving employees, and a turn of a phrase at the end that flattered their radio station and our organization at the same time which tied us together. I sent the letter, which quickly fell from my thoughts until a few weeks later when I was summoned to our front counter. I was stunned when two men introduced themselves as representatives from the radio station and told me that my team had been awarded the grand prize! I thanked them extensively and held the news from my folks until I could gather them all together.

When I corralled them and had their curiosity peaked, I relayed the details of the day at the beach and theme park. They were overwhelmed and quite amazed regarding the odds of this happening and the willingness to entertain the idea of entering on their behalf. As the excitement wound down somewhat, a flood of questions arose regarding logistics. As you can imagine, the most urgent problem commonplace to everyone at this juncture was, "Who's going to have to miss this day of fun because we can't all go – someone has to stay behind and work at our shop?" I was anticipating this. At this point, I reached into my bag of tools and brought out the one tool we managers possess, but some may never use it because they don't understand the impact it has upon your team and, in some cases, your legacy. I announced to them that I had arranged coverage from one of our other locations for that upcoming magical Friday in July and that I would remain in our location to oversee their successful administration of our daily tasks and assigned workload. There was some general scoffing at this paradigm. Not that they would be unable to function without their leader, but purely in disagreement with the notion that I had arranged this special event and yet would be self-precluded from enjoying and sharing it with them. As word spread throughout the other stores, I became a bit of a hero to some of those team members and some of my own. Taking one for the team, showing your humanity, or sometimes doing the right thing will garner a legion of fans and teammates who will often walk through fire for you down the road!

Give Them The Tools

If you are truly committed to running a successful business and desire a team that is empowered and poised to create and dominate as formidable leaders in whatever endeavor your organization declares to be important in their declared mission statement, then you absolutely must create and endorse a dedicated training program. I have had the great fortune of being employed early on in my career by an organization that held these beliefs in team member education and would dedicate the required resources to ensure that all trainings occurred in the proper timeframe and were mastered before that new hire was allowed to interact with equipment or clientele so as to never jeopardize the experience of either party.

The training model was of a classic four step design – prepare, present, try-out and follow-up. This style of hands-on learning allowed the trainee to review a detailed information sheet, brochure, binder etc. and then observe a fully competent trainer who demonstrated the exact proper and correct techniques required to be one hundred percent proficient in that skill. Once they have seen the demonstration(s), they are then given the opportunity to try their own hand at the task. Because they are actually allowed to touch the materials used to perform the task instead of merely observing their use by another or in a simulation on film, they immediately have a greater understanding of what is required to be successful. This tried-and-true method is preferred for training anyone on a new task where there is a necessity for physical touching for successful task completion. Whether we are flipping burgers, driving a snowplow, monitoring a ballot machine, throwing a baseball for the first time or feeding ourselves with a spoon while making the transition from the formula bottle to solid food, we all need to understand the concept, see it done successfully by a teacher and get our hands on it to try it for ourselves. We may drop some strained carrots on the floor the first time, but we will prevail with the support and necessary hand holding of a dedicated instructor.

Sadly, not every organization will allot the needed resources to ensure that an environment such as this exists within the framework of their businesses. Without question it is expensive in terms of labor budgets and staffing issues when the person instructing the new person is absent from the productive tasks normally performed by them when no training is needed. Much too often, training is the one item that is cut from the payroll budget projections when cash flow shortages occur in a business or when maneuvering toward a buyout or IPO. Everyone who has any business acumen realizes that the easiest course to make the bottom line look more attractive is to slash labor expenditures as the rewards are instantaneous and visible. Unfortunately, it is most often the human resources department that is first to experience the payroll slashing directives. Part of the HR group is inevitably the training team and as soon as they have been reassigned or let go, the official training program itself often goes by the wayside. This results in an increase in employee turnover as the newly hired persons are not properly inducted into the rigors and requirements of expected performance and wind up frustrated, unsure of their own performance and quite frequently resigning within a very short window of time. A new person is hired to replace them, and the cycle resumes with the "warm body syndrome" and a revolving door of potentially good teammates who never realize their own potential because no one took the time to introduce them to the job effectively. The manager becomes more desperate to fill the open positions and often skips or skimps on the proper sourcing, screening and hiring protocols resulting in poor decisions on the employment of someone to fill the spot. The performance of all parties suffers when this is allowed to transpire.

Obviously, the new hire is under-contributing as they aren't aware of what is expected or even possible in their role because they weren't shown and were merely thrown to the sharks in a sink or swim situation. The other team members will begin to tire of the confusion and incompetence of the new hires and will resent the additional workload they must shoulder to make up for that missing production. Their performance may very well diminish as a result and possible additional turnover is eminent and the effectiveness of the manager left holding the bag will be questioned and often irreparably harmed in the eyes of their team and perhaps the upper management. To complicate matters further, the manager most often has an added handicap in the correction of this vicious cycle because they, themselves, are forced to assume a front-line position on most days to help in picking up any slack created by this under (or poor) staffing debacle. They are caught in a no-win situation as they cannot openly criticize the decisions of the leaders and can only cajole their team to trudge forward until the prevailing winds of change blow again and training programs are restored as critical.

The other injured party in this fiasco that is so very often overlooked is the customer or client. Oftentimes, they do not reveal their displeasure with the current state of the service they are receiving (or lack thereof) and will quietly seek alternatives to remaining your business partner and discover another source to fulfill their needs. The true expense of replacing team members is substantially much greater than what would have been spent if the commitment to the training program had been maintained all along and the newly hired folks would have been allowed to take up the reins once they were indoctrinated and comfortable.

Training of new and existing team members is near and dear to my heart, and I've had the opportunity to instruct so very many during my career. One such series of classroom instruction I was blessed to develop was designed to fill a void in the officially designed company training program. In conjunction with my immediate supervisor, we designated a group of existing coworkers we believed were in possession of higher-level potential for promotion, expected to excel and hopefully lead the company in the not-too-distant future. They had, of course, undertaken all of the required company sponsored courses they needed to progress to the levels they had currently advanced to and were performing admirably, but nonetheless had gaps in their knowledge base.

I believe in a concept of knowledge that requires a little explanation to hopefully have it make sense to you, my reader. Let me try to explain. There are several levels of knowledge in my opinion. There is the information that you know. This includes all things taught or inherent to humans as a whole such as basic arithmetic, the pyramids are built in Egypt, or a skunk has a really awful odor. Then there is the knowledge that you do not know. This includes concepts (at least for me) such as how an automobile engine works, why do I get lost while driving despite GPS directions or what is the meaning of life and why are we here? This is the wisdom that you are aware that you are not in possession of and can aspire to learn, thus, uncovering the answers or specific knowledge to complete your deficiency. Now, there is another type of knowledge, and it was this type of information I desired to impart to this amazing group of students. This level of intelligence is one that we don't often consider if we ever do at all. It is the awareness of those ideas and perceptions regarding topics that we are unaware of our lack of knowledge or understanding of. Simply expressed as not knowing what we do not know. This is the unimaginable vastness of the universe in terms of how enormous this amount of unknown knowledge is. I equate it to landing on one page of the Google search engine and residing in the details of that realm as if it were the extent of all intelligence without ever having an inkling of the enormity of the knowledge that exists on the other unseen (unknown) pages. I make no claim that I am more intelligent than most of my peers and certainly do not possess the akashic record of knowledge but my goal with this group of students was to endow them with the information that would allow them to progress in their careers with our company that they may very well never accumulate as it was not included in the prescribed training materials. Many of the topics I have covered in this text were discussed along with many business specific idioms and the growth was amazing. Ideas associated with some obscure events they may encounter in the near future or perhaps never at all that they are now prepared for because they have been exposed to that level of thinking. Most items were intangible and certainly not addressed in any company training materials. Simply put – you don't know what you don't know. So many of these future leaders grew into long-term champions and tenured employees that ultimately stayed true to the organization, and many were promoted to higher management.

There is one last concept regarding training and the impact of not adhering to a dedicated program that I firmly believe to be true. I cannot take the credit for the origination of this tagline but will share it with you as it requires a little deeper thought and visualization to truly see the significance. "When the only tool in your tool belt is a hammer, you tend to view all problems as nails." If you don't tailor your response to the particulars of the event and have the ability to select from an unlimited choice of reactions, then you are destined to be ineffective as a leader. If you act upon every situation that arises in the arena you oversee as if it is an emergency and create an atmosphere of stress and panic until it is resolved, then your team will respond in the same manner. Every issue that arises for them will be met with a stressful and kneejerk response because they learned it from you. If, however, you manage to take a course of action that is tailored to the individual event, then your team will have the confidence that you can handle any and all situations whenever they might occur. You can give the appearance of "shooting from the hip" in many instances because of your understanding of the business model, events unfolding and people involved. All potential outcomes and pitfalls are understood. So well-practiced and honed by your prior experience and premeditated planning that you are very rarely caught off guard, thus providing the solid base on which your teams are built.

The example you set will be the behavior you can expect from those same teams. If you gossip, they will gossip. If you play favorites, they will become jealous and bickering adversaries undermining and backbiting each other and the cohesiveness of the group. If you are fair, consistent and clear in your expectations, they will respond in kind and have no concern of their own performance. A member of your team should never be surprised if they are given any performance counselling. If they are unaware of inappropriate conduct or underachievement in accomplishment of a task, then you are at fault because you either allowed them to proceed without correction or you failed to set the expectation prior to the beginning of the employment, project or circumstance. A leader that continues to grow in knowledge, skill and human resource management will never fall into the "one trick

pony" trappings and inspire many future business
pioneers.

Share The Wealth

Have you ever been on the other end of a conversation where a superior or peer was openly basking in the recognition being lauded by another onto them for an idea that clearly originated with you? How did that make you feel? I'm guessing that it left you feeling angry, sad, disappointed, deflated and unsure of who your true allies were. I have experienced this frustrating situation myself and I can attest that it's not a desirable occasion. I was stunned by my betrayal at the hands of a supervisor and held onto that infidelity throughout my remaining tenure under his jurisdiction. The relationship was damaged on my side, and I was never really sure of his motives moving forward. There was no monetary gain to be had and perhaps his thought process was unintentional, and he never realized his over-stepping in announcement of this idea but ultimately, the line was crossed, and I withdrew from further discussions of potential ideas with him. Maybe I should have confronted him and expressed my disappointment and demanded he readdress the topic with the supervisor and give the credit for the suggestion to me. I preferred instead, to take the higher road. Either way the relationship was damaged.

It is critical that as a leader, you acknowledge the ideas and suggestions submitted to you by your team members either verbally or in writing and offer feedback upon the validity of those thoughts. Once you have determined whether there is feasibility to the suggestion, then you must either inform them that you don't believe it's a viable solution at this juncture or that you believe it has merit and you would wish to present it through the proper channels for consideration with their approval. If they agree upon submission, then the moment is ripe for ensuring that all credit for the concept is awarded to them. If the referral of the idea occurs during a planned or unexpected visit by an upper-level management representative, then it should be introduced and referenced to your employee. Whenever possible, the inclusion of them in the discussion and the specified notation of the origin of the submission is preferable. Inviting the teammate into the normally closed circle will automatically inflate their self-esteem and allow them to enjoy the commentary and hopefully accolades of the leader that is usually beyond their league. As the person that they look to as their protector and in some cases, shield from the corporate emissaries, you have the opportunity to cement their loyalty and unquestioning faith in your leadership. Again, do the right and just thing.

There are times however, when you have to be "that guy." In the role of leadership and responsibility, there are moments when you simply have to be the boss and cannot instead be the hero. If you have clearly established the policies and procedures that are to be adhered to always, then it is also your duty to respond to any and all violations with swift and deliberate punishment for transgressions. Tardiness, fraud, timeclock falsifications, theft, missed deadlines, discrimination, slander, workplace violence and insubordination to name just a few are misconduct that require your immediate attention. The act of delaying your response (unless directed by your supervisor or HR representative if serious enough) or indecision on your course of action can cost you credibility and respect in the eyes of those aware of the infraction. It may very well signal the sanctioning of similar misdeeds for the perpetrator and others who may have been considering such attempts but had been unsure of your attention and potential response. Expedited and decisive investigation and doling out of discipline is critical to preserving the image of the untainted director.

The investigation into the matter should include only those with a stake in the event or offense. This meeting should not include other past delinquencies or suspicions that have been on the "clipboard" and could easily become additional fodder for the confrontation about to take place. If the matter at hand is regarding the deliberate falsification of a timeclock punch, the suspicion of theft of someone else's food from the breakroom refrigerator should not be attached just because you have a "while we are at it" attitude. You might wish to unpack any dislike you may harbor regarding this particular individual but now is not the time. Instead, the interview must be held in private with only the most necessary people present. It is always a strong suggestion to have at least one other non-biased and non-peer representative attend as well so the conversation that transpires cannot be mis-interpreted and devolve into a "he said – she said" contention.

Prepare for the discussion with facts and evidence and present those without emotion or allowing for nor accepting excuses. By utilizing the "headfirst" strategy outlined in an earlier chapter, you ensure that there is no chance of allowing anything but your desired declaration to be stated clearly and with no possibility for misunderstanding nor lessening of the offense and its forthcoming consequences. If you believe there is a chance for violence, make sure to allow for a clear path between the associate and the door to the room you choose for interrogation. Never present an environment that can be construed as confinement for both legal and personal safety reasons. Lay the facts on the table, have an agenda of remarks you intend to make and state the consequences so all involved will understand the events which will be put into motion once the meeting concludes. It may be simply a notation in the employee's employment file with a promise of more severe consequences administered if the offense were to recur within an allotted timeframe. At the other extreme, this may result in immediate termination of employment if the infraction is of a nature serious enough to warrant that action or prior warnings have been violated by this new misconduct. Most companies in this modern era will make every effort to protect the employee from indiscriminate discipline and abuse at the hands of an under-skilled and often undertrained leader. Most have progressive discipline programs in place to ensure that proper legal steps have been taken prior to any termination of staff members to avoid potential litigation from disgruntled employees believing they were let go for insufficient cause. This second set of eyes being trained on the facts of the alleged misdeed is for your benefit as well in assuring you have all your "ducks in a row," and are correct in your decision to terminate or administer severe discipline. Desiring avoidance of this potential backlash after the termination of an employee, the effective manager follows the policies in place regarding employment, productivity and workplace expectations. They deliberately outline all of this information to their teams and all new hires. They consistently and strictly adhere to rigid observation of this doctrine at all times and address any violations swiftly and without prejudice or favoritism. By doing so, every team member has a sense of belonging and belief that they are an equal part of something bigger than themselves or their manager.

Bringing an end to someone else's career was never one of the managerial tasks that I enjoyed. I have known some who relished the assignment and eagerly awaited the moment when they could drop the axe. Although it wasn't a function I personally enjoyed and in reality, dreaded in most cases, I understood the importance of performing the obligation professionally, succinctly and with empathy. I was never a cold-hearted robotic administrator of the delivery of someone's walking papers, but I approached each session with one truism in mind. They did this to themselves – I did not. Poor decisions are made by our teams on occasion and oftentimes, they get caught in the fallout of their actions. They brought the consequences down upon themselves and as the representative of the organization, the responsibility rests solely upon the manager's shoulders to take the required actions to address the infraction. There is no gray area here. Perform what must transpire or resign yourself to being an ineffective, disrespected, namby pamby who will be walked all over by the staff they are charged to direct.

There was a time when I was asked to assume leadership of a very troubled location of the national pharmacy chain I was currently employed by. Having been employed by the direct competitor of this chain, I was taken aback by the stark differences in business philosophy and operation of my new employer. They were two of the top three pharmacy conglomerates but they were at opposite ends of the spectrum in terms of treatment of personnel and facilities. This site was in a very depressed section of town and was crime-riddled and staffed with undertrained and in some cases, dishonest employees. I agreed to a transfer and began what became a career-lasting succession of quick-fix rebuilding of such stores. I was branded as the "go-to" manager assigned to clean up, re-staff and transform underperforming stores until I found more agreeable employment elsewhere. I became known as the "axe man" because I terminated so very many existing co-workers within the locations I was remaking. It was a title I was averse to because I much prefer to build up a team employing positive actions and not through attrition and dictatorial measures. It dawned upon me in short measure that the troubles within these places of business were brought on by the policies and practices of the corporate offices. The treatment of the employees was deplorable. There was no trust, no training, no paths for advancement. In short – no hope. Is there really any wonder as to why the employees behaved the way they did? The saddest aspect still is that after I was reassigned to the next "hell hole," the company would assign an inexperienced manager (or in some cases assistant manager) to lead the team in my wake with the sole purpose of lessening payroll. As you can imagine, it was not long until the site returned to the condition it had been in prior to my resurrection of it.

Nonetheless, I toiled for two to six months in location after location until I became so disenchanted with the corporate workings of that company and began to look elsewhere. I will freely admit that there were a small handful of former coworkers that I did take the smallest amount of pleasure in the administration of their termination. One in particular had her nametag burned in effigy by the teammates she left behind upon termination. Sometimes nothing can lift the spirits of your team more than a change in membership and the removal of someone who has acted as a cancerous growth upon the unity of the group. Once they have departed, the overall mood and productivity can skyrocket even if it presents a staff "shortage." Somehow, they become oblivious to that deficiency until quite a while has passed and by then a new hire is in the stages of becoming a welcome addition.

The team leader is also a human being beneath the Superman/Clark Kent disguise. As such, it is also vital that you bring your humanity into your everyday managerial role. Textbook and company handbook leadership and rule adherence is paramount as I've stated but you also must have a heart for your teammates. Understanding that they are people first and employees second is crucial. The young individual who only last evening was dumped from the only true romantic relationship they have ever been involved in, will not perform as well today on the production floor as they have on any day prior. The tenured gentleman who has been your rock when it comes to client negotiations will not be as authentic and detailed on the day after discovering his wife has a diagnosis of late-stage cancer and his world has been shattered. The customer who has been an absolutely wonderful business partner for many years will suddenly ferociously complain about your service after a small mistake because she has been told her position is being eliminated in a few weeks and she will be let go. When these unexpected occurrences crop up in your daily routines, there must be a temperament within you that can find a muted response to the deviance from the norm. The rule states that the behavior requires some form of discipline, and it does, but the key is to mete out the punishment to fit the merits of the crime and the circumstances that triggered the unusual behavior. You may need to employ tactics that you had never thought of before. Maybe a short leave of absence can prevent additional disciplinary actions because after a few days the youngster's heart will start to heal, and they can return their attention to the requirements of the job. Maybe allowing the depressed and despondent coworker time to reach out to professional, company sponsored counselling services or health care treatment options will prevent a complete collapse of their otherwise exemplary work history. Your long-term customer may benefit from an employment site you have used to source applicants in the past or perhaps you are currently seeking additional staffing yourself. The point being, consistency in your actions is vital, but there are occasions when the box is not always square, and solutions may be hiding in one of those oddly shaped corners.

The BBC produced an enjoyable television series titled Mr. Selfridge in 2013-2016 comprising 40 episodes recounting the real-life story of the flamboyant American founder of a department store in the heart of London in the early 1900's. His personal affairs may be distasteful, but many of his practices and policies regarding the daily operation of his grand retail spectacle are similar to those I profess. Additionally, the treatment of his employees is (for the most part) supportive of those I embrace. One episode in particular brought me to tears. He is informed of theft by a trusted employee. They catch her red-handed and call her out before her peers (that part I emphatically disagree with), and he emotionally addresses the assembled team and passionately reasserts his philosophy that they are an inter-reliant "family" and that what she did was a betrayal to the team and to him personally. You can feel the emotion in him as he has taken this perceived treachery so personally. She expresses that she stole to feed her ailing mother and he finds himself in the toughest of positions. To follow policy and set an example or to excuse her behavior and give her another chance. He decided to terminate her employment and release her without a reference. No reference virtually makes her undesirable to other potential employers in that Victorian era, and she becomes destitute. Mr. Selfridge is made aware of her situation yet affirms his position and declines again to issue a reference so she might find work. Warning – spoiler ahead. She commits suicide and leaves him a letter stating how much she enjoyed working for him and apologizes for her mistake and holds no anger toward him. She had nothing to live for as her mother had passed and she wished to join her in the afterlife. He, however, is crushed as you can imagine. Form your own opinions, but I for one found myself in those shoes and it is the most difficult role you have as leader.

Guidelines to Understanding

To be successful, certain truths are a necessity for your team to rely upon in understanding that their individual worth and contribution to the group as a whole are valuable and intrinsic. Violating these hypotheses can often result in the deterioration of faith and trust and the disillusionment of corporate integrity by the stakeholders. Some promises carry a heavier weight than others, but collectively, the results are the same. An organization that aspires to fulfill this mantra will be viewed by its team members as deliberately more ethical and incorruptible than its counterpart, wherein deceit, lies, and malicious acts are allowed to thrive and become everyday worries for the employees.

They are sharing the vision. It is critical that every team member understands the "big picture" and recognizes the status of progress toward the stated goal and the worthiness of any proposed effort to achieve that goal. If they don't grasp the importance of their role and any tasks they are assigned in the direction of the main objective, then they will not be fully vested in that task and merely "kill time" or "spin their wheels." Those goals must encompass the S.M.A.R.T methodology in keeping them Specific, Measurable, Achievable, Relevant, and Time-bound. Learning to Create goals using this method is fodder for someone else's classroom or instruction from another anthology or training environment. Suffice it to say, that topic has been examined beyond exhaustion, and models and methods abound on-line. Most goals, however, are decided with a superb desire to benefit only a tiny percentage of those involved and are unrealistic at best. To arbitrarily invoke a demand for a 10, 20, 30, 40, or 50 percent increase in sales year-over-year without the "how-to" steps is unattainable in most instances and impossible if it's just someone in management "wishing" it to happen. It's still okay to dream of fantastic success in business and team development, but the dream must be based on reality, and the plan has to be concrete. Visualize the ultimate achievement, strategize on the details, determine its legitimacy in potential achievement, and reevaluate the process to adhere to the realized adjustments, then relay the plan to the team. The final step in the process is ensuring the "buy-in" of your team. Most employees listen to WII-FM, and you must solve the "what's in it for me?" question they all bring to the table. The answer to that question can vary significantly from a simple, engaging pizza party to profit-sharing incentives or prizes awarded. If everyone can envision the achievement of the goal, then everyone will climb aboard, and others may still see their involvement as potential for career advancement.

<u>Empowerment</u>. You are empowering them and letting them fly without fear of bumping into the ceiling of their granted authority. While building a cohesive team, it becomes necessary to instill decision-making authority upon one, some, or all of your employees (unless you wish to be called upon every time someone needs to go to the bathroom). Those who have demonstrated a willingness and talent for discerning the best outcome from a given set of circumstances will rise to the forefront of your group and be the obvious choice(s) for leadership roles. Others may also exhibit some ability and desire and should be rewarded with lesser decision-making responsibility. Most of these associates will accept this capacity, interpreting it as a privilege to be involved and empowered to resolve more minor issues. Once these tiers of authority have been established, the very worst thing you can do is step into a situation they have been presented with and, without allowing them to ascertain the solution themselves, direct the outcome yourself before they can do so. Stepping upon their toes and undermining their ability to perform in the role of decision-maker renders them impotent before they can ever discern their leadership proficiency. They may forever second guess any future decision and often bring that to you because you have demonstrated to them that despite placing them in a position of authority, you never truly believed they were capable. By usurping their supposed power, you have effectively rendered them powerless. Empower them and then stand back. If they decide on a solution vastly different from what you would have implemented, teach them by utilizing that example, incorporating a "maybe next time" mentality. Since they know the parameters and policies of the organization, it is doubtful that they will offer redress that is out of line, given the specifics of the circumstances. In some instances, you may become the student and find that your protégé responded to the occurrence in a manner you wouldn't have considered and that their response was, in fact, a more satisfactory solution for all parties concerned. Information and education flow in both directions in a healthy organization and nothing should be discounted just because they originated in the mailroom or at the entry level.

<u>Respect</u> is a two-way street. In the workplace, managers often believe that their title alone will ensure the respect and devotion of those they supervise. Nothing could be further from the truth. The manager can frequently be the brunt of employee jokes, snide remarks, back-talk, and complaints around the water cooler or in general conversation. If there is little or no respect for the person in charge, then that individual's effectiveness and usually tenure are likely to be deficient and short-lived. Those megalomaniacs will scream and curse and loudly reinforce their own self-proclamation of authority in an audience of employees who know the reality of their credibility. Once their windbag has been emptied and they return to the hiding place they call an office, the authentic leadership reassumes its control, and the laughter returns at the expense of the "boss." Usually, the only individual who cannot perceive this debacle is the one who is purportedly in command of the operation. Sometimes, the team performs well enough despite this inept leader, and the upper management may not recognize the ineffectiveness of their appointed commander before the real damage is done. Suppose this ineffective team director receives even the smallest corporate accolades for the efforts performed by their team (acting without their direction). In that case, the unrecognized and unofficial leaders may mutiny and desert that supervisor. If this happens, exposure of the manager's weakness is virtually assured, but at the expense of well-trained and valuable team members.

To establish respectability with your team, honesty, and trust must be built. Having been in management roles with several gigantic organizations, one consistency has remained. The team you are about to inherit or make will primarily be concerned with how you conduct yourself and your demeanor when interacting with them. Operational strategies and goals will also be necessary to them, but nothing exceeds their concern regarding what type of leader you will be daily. Will you deliver direction from your office through an underling, scream, and yell from the production floor, or will you stand beside them and lead them to success through firm and gentle guidance?

Some perceive themselves as less of a headmaster if they are not on a mounted steed or raining down boiling oil from their office's castle battlements. Lord Acton mused, "Absolute power corrupts absolutely," in some cases, the same can be applied to those promoted to the position of management. Somewhere along the path, the notion of fair play and democracy in the

workplace was replaced with the idea that the only accurate leadership methodology is one in which the supervisors themselves wield the only authority and command from a distance with a disdain for interpersonal involvement. How absurd!
Others believe they are only effective if they can maintain a hovering leadership in which they don't get their hands dirty like those they oversee. They might be effective in their planning and direction, but there is no "buy-in" or deep respect emanating from their teams. They want to distance themselves somewhat and not get "too close" to those they rely upon to move the organization forward for fear they might have to discipline, which would present conflict with their personality. Those team members understand that although their leader presents an outward appearance of integrity, they do not truly "belong" and would not sacrifice themselves for the whole. They see the team members as dispensable and subject to replacement or upgrade should the need arise. There would be no tears shed should that transpire.

There is not anything inherently despicable in this approach that I can see. It is, however, in my opinion, less effective as a leadership model. To truly gain the respect of those who comprise your work mates, you must be fully vested in them. This means removing the rose-colored glasses and seeing them with all their blemishes and quirks. It requires empathy when hurt or during great turmoil in their lives—joyfully celebrating the events they present to you with gusto and enthusiasm - not as if you are part of their immediate family but because you have become just that. They do not accept excuses that belittle your relationship as boss and subordinate but are open to the belief that they can rise above that distinction and genuinely present you with the truth because they respect you that much as a person and not as their employer.

Let me relate a case in point. A twenty-five-year employee reported to me during the last six of those years. He became one of my most trusted team members, was heavily relied upon to perform many administrative tasks, and had terrific interpersonal skills with our client base. Nearly every customer that phoned asked for him by name. He was an "institution" in our location and was well-recognized throughout the district amongst other employees working within different divisions. He was a reference for newer team members on training and operational questions and those from nearby locations. He and I developed a very close relationship and shared some personal histories regarding ourselves. This was commonplace with many of the crew within that site, as they had been together years before my arrival and were very close-knit. My relationship with them all was much more relaxed than most of my prior experiences, and I credit them for many of the location's successes. We often enjoyed a laugh and attended some external activities together. When I muddled through a divorce after a twenty-five-year marriage, he was right there to help pick me up and offer consolation and a source of needed comic relief. It came to my attention while investigating the suspicious dealings of one of my newer employees via a video recording that my trusted team member was violating a policy that was a terminable offense. I reviewed the evidence again to ensure I hadn't misinterpreted it and interviewed my trusted coworker. He freely admitted to the acts captured by surveillance video. He explained that he was helping out an unemployed friend by allowing him to use our product without charge, thinking there was no actual monetary or very minimal loss for the company. I had uncovered this violation by stumbling upon it. It never would have crossed my mind that he might be violating trust. My trust. If I excused it and neglected to act upon it, no one would ever know outside the two of us. We could resume our relationship, and our operation would return to its regular functionality. No one would be subjected to a staff shortage, nor would that precious resource be lost to all the current and future team members. I looked at him and informed him that he was immediately terminated and would need to leave the premises after cleaning his locker. He shook my hand and said he completely understood and was apologetic for his actions but realized he had erred and was prepared to accept the punishment.

To this day, he and I are still very close friends. On a side note, the team member I was initially investigating was also terminated by me on the same day for theft, which had also been uncovered with the video review. I ended up short two staff members in one hour. Ironically, that teammate was apologetic for the foolish decision he had made as well and thanked me for the opportunity and his time spent on our team. He occasionally visited and said hello to those he left behind until he permanently left the area. When you establish mutual respect within the workplace, even a terrible interaction can be understood and treated professionally. No doubt, emotions may come into play, but moving forward in an honest and ethically correct direction is paramount. Of course, an invisible line must be drawn between employee and supervisor, but those skilled managers can dance on that line without being tripped by it.

Aces In Their Places

In the development of any team, confident, natural leaders will inherently rise to the top. They might require a degree of encouragement and, of course, further training and development, but instinctively, they will demonstrate the attributes that you will find suitable to aid in directing your organization toward its stated objectives. These natural gifts are desirable traits that often percolate below the surface and can be unearthed with some delicate probing or with the unexpected emersion of the individual into an unforeseen situation in which a solution is required without the consultation of a supervisor. They may surprise themselves with this unknown talent and can grow this latent skill from a seedling with just minor encouragement from you. Once the ripening has occurred, you can continue to offer training, advice, and skill-sharpening techniques to develop their proficiency further. When these inherent gifts become evident, the successful manager will recognize them for what they are, assign appropriate tasks that complement their intrinsic talents, and avoid counterintuitive duties. The poor leader will try to quash and devalue the emerging abilities, primarily out of jealousy and perhaps fear of lessening their self-importance. If drastic enough, the fledgling talents may be re-submerged and never allowed to blossom again by the employee because they are embarrassed, debased, and reluctant to go out on that limb again. Sad, but often the result of leaders who defy (deny) the internal growth of their teams and stifle development.

The same can be said for other skills that do not necessarily require leadership ability but require more technical, mechanical, or artistic productivity. Suppose a team member who has demonstrated proficiency in designing and implementing an airplane seating upgrade is suddenly given the task of training the pilots regarding the flight instrument panel. In that case, the chances of success are slim to none. They most likely do not possess that skill set or, at best, may understand the basics but have never been afforded the opportunity for training and practice. However, that is not to say that the coworker might not desire to acquire that additional knowledge and perhaps one day become that flight panel instructor. Still, nowadays, they are not qualified and should not be presented with the responsibility of performing those tasks. Always listen to and monitor the desired career advancements of the team. Suppose the team member states a new career aspiration option during an informal discussion or while developing an Individual Development Plan (IDP). In that case, every effort must be undertaken to ensure that ambition is viable. There is no such thing as an over-trained or overambitious team member. The greater their knowledge, the greater their possibilities for success. Again, I refer back to the megalomaniac who believes that success will occur only if they determine every step, handle every obstacle, be present at every turn, makes every decision, and accept all the accolades. That is a recipe for disaster; your teams will not support you in the long run.

Regardless of the operation you oversee, you must ensure that your most skilled team members are positioned in the roles in which they can excel and will render the greatest asset to your client base because of that placement. The organization will thrive and grow when the roles are clear, and the responsibilities are shared so that all parties involved believe their contributions are valued and recognized by their peers. Creating an environment where daily ambiguity about what tasks and assignments each person will be expected to perform causes undue stress and anxiety for everyone. The managers themselves cannot plan beyond the moment, for there is never the click, click,

click of a smoothly operating team in which they can look beyond the immediate and focus on the anticipated. If there is a frequent and demanding interruption to your planning to put out the fires that ignite, then there will be no concise course-setting for tomorrow because you cannot escape today. Tomorrow will bring more of the same, and success will remain a fleeting ideal that will always be beyond reach. Instead, if tomorrow you assign your aces in their proper places and empower them to perform without requiring frequent interruption and distraction from the duties and tasks you must complete, you will find yourself at the end of the day with a solid plan. Not just for tomorrow but for a time far in the future and all the days leading up to it. No person can foresee all events, and an agenda designed to prevent this type of current chaos in which you reside is paramount if you desire a rewarding career that can be ulcer-free. Your team and your customers deserve the expectation of a comfortable interaction every time they enter the premises. Consistency of assignment, consistency of product generated, consistency of the property's appearance, consistency of expectation, and consistency of their manager's actions. No surprises.

One of the most potent responses a manager can give when presented with an employee inquiry is that they do not know the answer. To admit that you are unaware of the desired information serves to level the playing field somewhat in their eyes and humanize you slightly more. Managers are often considered all-knowing and infallible, but we are people just like everyone else. It's akin to asking one of your schoolteachers a question and stumping them for an answer. It is somewhat unnerving that this individual who has always presented themselves as the possessor of all information regarding the subject matter they are credited with mastering is left scratching their head for the desired response. Like the student, the employee will anxiously await your reaction to this problem. As the supervisor, you can follow up with this in several ways. The most effective course of action is to state that although you are unaware of the solution, you will assume the responsibility to seek that unknown information and report back as soon as you have determined it after utilizing all available resources. Another option is to inquire about their ideas regarding a possible answer. They may have developed a perfect solution and presented the originating dilemma to you to gauge additional thinking before moving forward with their suggestion. By doing so, they can assess if the situation has arisen before and what the outcome was or, if new, whether you might generate a more advanced solution before they extend themselves for possible rebuke. The third possible response is that the proffered inquiry is unimportant and not worth dwelling upon simply because you do not desire to reveal your ignorance or deem it worthy of your time. Shutting down an employee without due process results in their reluctance to present any future inquiries, suggestions, or ideas that may have otherwise been beneficial to your organization.

Last In - First Out

Absolutely nothing will win over the loyalty of your employees more significant than the demonstration of rolling up one's sleeves and diving into the hornet's nest of activity currently permeating your front line. Whether it's taking a customer's order, fielding a complaint, wiping up a spillage, unloading a truck, or merely answering a ringing telephone, the impression of granting some relief to others makes the gesture more appreciated. The willingness to jump into the fray and sacrifice attention from the duties usually assigned to you engenders and promotes a one-for-all and all-for-one mentality in the organization. When they witness you toiling alongside them, then suddenly, the burden is less because those at the top care about the struggles of the underlings. Your sincerity in this effort requires genuine interest and the desire to aid their unanticipated flurry of activity. Any attempt to make an "appearance" amongst them merely to give the impression that you are helping out as "one of the guys" will be quickly unmasked and understood for exactly the grandstanding that it is. Rhetorical and dogmatic attempts at being trustworthy while secretly desiring to enhance your image are despicable and have no place in any workplace.

Occasionally, a situation such as this will arise. As you witness it, you must decide whether to enter the struggle and what task you'll assume will deliver the most significant assistance to the team. You must answer the obvious question - what is the expense to the other items you must also accomplish from your own "to-do" list? Suppose you elect to roll up your sleeves and get involved. In that case, you must always adhere to the adage that as the team leader, you have other responsibilities that revolve around higher-level, longer-term objectives; therefore, you are obligated by that responsibility never to allow yourself to become bogged down by these additional tasks you take on. Because you cannot afford to put on a pair of blinders similar to those your team often wears while task-saturated, you are advised to follow the rule of being the last person on the team to abandon your assigned position and the first person to break away from that temporary task to resume your managerial role. Any other course of action would be foolish. Those you supervise will become dependent upon your inability to distinguish between the appropriate need for your assistance and when the team can function well enough without you while you continue your required tasks. You will experience a multitude of team members who bring various levels of self-direction. The more self-assured of these will make every attempt to complete all necessary tasks regardless of workload and aspire to create an environment in which they rarely, if ever, require your assistance. They feel they have failed you and are quick to address any topics you bring to their attention and send you back to your office. These are the greatest assets to you and will allow your ultimate success. Often, the best course of action is no action at all. Allowing them to find their answers can be the best team-building activity possible. The key, however, is knowing the difference and exactly when to intervene. Furthermore, you must be sure that by diving into the action, you have not missed the opportunity to be of more excellent aid by taking actions that would alleviate future similar occurrences. Perhaps a schedule modification, promotion of a team member to supervisor, recruiting and hiring, and training a replacement for a departed coworker might be time better spent and could lay the foundation for avoiding future issues.

On the other end of the spectrum, you will encounter team members who require what I always called "babysitting." I mean them no disrespect by this term, but it represents the state where you will find yourself regarding daily interactions with them. They nearly always need reassurance at the beginning of their day that they have value and are visible to their peers. They do this by bringing in an outside event that impacted them in some manner to elicit advice or just attention from others. The venting is usually quite bland but is presented in a manner that embellishes the degree of drama involved. There is a good deal of eye-rolling behind this person's back from the other team members, which is usually good-natured and often somewhat endearing as these coworkers recognize the dramatics as non-threatening and perhaps even enjoyable. It's a sort of comic relief before the rigors of the day.

Beyond this simple behavior, however, often exists a more profound insecurity, which becomes evident when, as their manager, you are called upon frequently and excitedly to assist them with everyday occurrences that they have often experienced, if not daily. It becomes irrelevant how often you give the solution and remind them of its origin and where the answer can be found on their own because, regardless, they will persist in requesting your guidance and facilitation every time. After all, it represents comfort and assurance to them. These individuals are often some of your best performers despite the frustration with the nearly constant time-consuming attention they crave. Unless they are inadequate in performing the functional requirements of the position, you are obligated to be the babysitter.

Most teams I've been associated with have had a combination of all the various personality types and, in being so, have performed admirably. As managers, we often have many under our watchfulness who have experienced less-than-desirable home lives or have run afoul of their biological parents and have lost that nurturing relationship. They flounder in some areas and, in many cases, latch onto you because you represent a solid foundation on which they can build their individuality and a source they can look to for advice and guidance. In the span of my career, I have had so many "adopted" children that my extended family is gigantic, and I wouldn't want it any other way. Most of the issues and dilemmas presented were minor, and a short dialogue and affirmation were required to relieve their anxiety and allow them to perform their duties as needed. Occasionally, a more severe predicament would arise, and additional thought and advice would be necessary to aid them. Several times, the directive was to pursue the answer with a professional counselor or direct them to reestablish contact with a family member, which was relevant and necessary. Faith and trust in you are what brings them to your door, so it's with these two virtues that your response can be encased. Be there for them, and you will find that they will always be there for you.

I have been instructed in training and "how-to" manuals that you should not surround yourself with people who resemble you. I understand this mindset from a diversity-forward mentality and a creative perspective. More so than ever before, the workplace has the advantage of diversity and inclusion. This has been too long overdue, and although advances have been made, there is still a long way to go. Company hiring practices have often been a reflection of the hiring manager bringing onboard individuals that look like them, talk like them, share the same values, and offer no additional life experience outside what the prototype possesses. With increased diversity, the company is open to the expansion of ideas for the betterment of the staff, customers, and, often, the environment. Opportunities are available for under-represented people outside of what may have been traditionally the make-up of that organization in the past.

Additionally, that organization's potential for creativity and innovation increases tremendously, and greater prosperity awaits at every turn. I wholeheartedly agree with this hiring strategy and have strived to create a diverse workforce in every position I've held, and I believe I was successful. Often, the staff would sway from male-dominated to female-dominated just because of the sourced applicants at that particular snapshot in time and be representative of various races, cultures, creeds, and orientations. On every team, however, there was always that one individual who "got me" in learning the minutiae and particulars of how I preferred all aspects of the location. A few special folks come to mind when I consider this. One was an assistant manager I worked with in the pharmacy business. She understood my idiosyncrasies so well that I merely had to suggest a task, and she would perform it so well that I was not inclined to adjust any part of it. She treated our team members the same way that I would. She was simply amazing! When I moved on to a different organization, I had an opportunity to offer her a position with the new company, and fortunately, she agreed to come onboard. Not surprisingly, it was a very short period before she was promoted to the position of branch manager.
It is critical to listen to your team members and acknowledge their suggestions. It is also vital that you continue your education and take advantage of the differences they bring to the table so you can expand your horizons of thought. Incorporate this influx of novel ideas into your long-term planning and cultivate an individual (or several) who can envision your strategy and become your clone to assist in its continual accomplishment.

Rules Of Engagement

Some events occasionally transpire that one of your team members may believe violate the acceptable behavioral standards of your workplace, and they demand to register a grievance. The offender may have been one of their peers, a vendor, a customer, or a management team member; proper handling and expeditious response is essential. As such, they must also follow the "chain of command." Put, an offense perpetrated by a peer should be reported to the supervisor of both parties and not reported (immediately) to the organization's CEO. The seriousness of the transgression is best determined by the individual experiencing the recipient end of the action, and reporting should come from such a person. The response of the supervisor receiving the information should immediately ease the anxiety or anger of the affronted party with the assurance of action.

Those actions can be as little as a private admonishment of the offender (if warranted) to an investigation involving all concerned individuals. Regardless of the depth of the research required, the aggrieved person must be confident that they will be afforded justice to some degree. Failure of the supervisor to act in a timely fashion or their inaction warrants the escalation of the issue to the level above their particular station. Any lack of actual or perceived concern will determine how your team adheres to the chain of command and its utilization of the prescribed escalation path when an issue exists. They will always take the preferred resolution route if the response is effective and timely. Still, suppose they believe it to be covered up or whitewashed by their immediate directors. In that case, they will skip over levels and report the injustice further above in the hierarchy -

essentially undermining the authority of those they report to. Exposure to a broken support system will usually lower respect for the management team. It may even cause reassignment, replacement, or termination due to inappropriate behavior and lack of confidence by upper management. The likelihood of bringing the team back into the fold without one or more of these changes is unlikely. Your boss should never ask you why one of your team members calls them. It's all about trust, and if they don't have faith in your genuine commitment to their overall well-being and interest, they will be intolerant of any perceived lack of such.

There needs to be a predetermined set of expectations that bind you as a manager to the team and the team as individuals and collectively to you and each other regarding the daily interactions amongst everyone. So many disruptions and conflicts arise in the workplace because of misheard gossip, misdirected instruction, misinformed hearsay, misaligned allegiance, misunderstood intentions, etc., because clear rules of engagement are non-existent. I used to **joke** that I wouldn't hire any more young ladies because we had too many on staff now with Miss Direction, Miss Understanding, Miss Placement, Miss Informed, Miss Handle, Miss Construed, Miss Read... (chuckle, chuckle). A few of these promises set in stone and adhered to by the team can go a long way toward avoiding harmful situations into which your team may fall—seeking understanding when unsure of your interpretation of events or communication is essential. Asking the message's source or action for clarification cannot be overstated. Seeking the answer from a third party will most likely result in less than total clarity and often result in a taking-of-sides mentality. Upon rendering the intended intention, immediate feedback to the giver is encouraged to assure understanding and arrest any inequities fleshed out.

Essential to this process is the steadfastness of a two-way conversation. This cannot be allowed to denigrate into a one-way yelling match where one or the other dominates in expressing their views at the exclusion or overspeak of the others. Angry confrontation benefits no one and certainly will be detrimental to harmony within the team if allowed to go unchecked when it arises. Like two boxers, parties need to be refereed and sometimes sent back to their corners until they can cool down and come out amiably talking instead of swinging. Every point of contention has many facets that can be explored collectively until a reasonable compromise can be reached. It often becomes the manager's role to serve as mediator and judge to ensure that a solution acceptable to all parties can be attained. You may need to decide if the parties cannot agree to a resolution. In such cases, impartiality and adherence to policies should dictate the judgment.

Presenting your determination to all concerned parties should both quell the dispute and set a precedent for future disagreement. At this juncture, remind the parties of the proper chain of command and their option to take it to the next level if they are dissatisfied with your settlement decision. An interesting side note to this topic is this. I have observed on several occasions that anger breeds productivity. By this, I mean that when one employee is upset with another or a group of teammates, they tend to "put their nose to the grindstone" and produce more work than their usual allotment. The others involved may do likewise; the atmosphere is dark and gloomy, with high tensions rising. No one likes to work under these circumstances, and an environment where the mood is light and friendly is much more conducive to long-term harmony. A manager who attempts to harness the power of this rivalry or pit one team member against another to capitalize on this forced concentration of effort will not be rewarded with an enjoyable career and will quickly alienate almost everyone on his team.

It is also important that no party or parties walk away from this adjudication with any "egg on their face." Embarrassment of your team member(s) will result in unhealthy and undesirable outcomes. A disgruntled coworker can disrupt the fabric of teamwork and quietly or secretly toil toward the failure of others while harboring their anger or resentment because of the public humiliation they believe they endured. The sad truth is that this perceived self-chagrin is often entirely within their minds as it had been forgotten by most of the team who had moved on in "victory" long ago. Whatever the situation, that teammate may experience performance issues, get involved with policy violations, and ultimately resign or be terminated.

Ridicule and shame are powerful weapons used by bullies and can never be acceptable in the workplace. As the supervisor, not only must you create an environment where this can never occur, but you must also be the stalwart example of refraining from participation in jest at the expense of any team member. We believe sometimes that assistant managers or those above us on the corporate ladder can be held in confidence and allow ourselves to engage in off-color behavior or merriment without the thought of it being observed by another and related to the party indicated as the object of ridicule. An assistant can often walk both sides of the fence with the team, so they sometimes reveal entrusted information believed to be less important; they desire to appear both in the "know" of management level information and yet still a member of the peers from which they were most likely promoted. They fail to understand the degree of damage they can create with off-the-cuff remarks. A wise manager refrains from any temptation to participate in such commentary and discourages it among their management team. An ounce of prevention is worth a pound of cure. A cure might not even be possible if a team member has experienced ridicule - especially at the hands of a previously respected and trusted leader.

Two words can renew an environment that has become awful to those subjected to work within into one much more comfortable and offer renewed hope for cohesion. "I'm sorry." In the role of manager, when we discover that we are incorrect regarding an idea, policy, or philosophy we espoused before the team, the most desirable course of action is to admit your error and ask for forgiveness by simply saying, "I'm sorry." This admission of regret can be triggered by an event, statement, or action that occurred recently or in the remote past. The timeframe of the action is less important. If you uncover information today that excuses an action of a team member from the past that exonerates them from the proposed misdeed, then there should be a redress of the error publicly or privately. Even though they may never discover this new information on their own, you owe it to them to delete it from their record. If it was something you said and now have had a change of belief, allow them absolution through revelation of your reassessed conviction. Proffering an acknowledgment of misjudgment or inaccuracy will increase your humility, ethical steadfastness, and sincerity in the eyes of your team. To err is human; we are all subjected to the occasional mistake and need to atone for it to not only correct the record but also to keep the atmosphere clear of suspicion, misunderstanding, or mistrust.

As the leader, you are responsible for providing a workplace free of contempt, fear, gossipmongering, envy, bullying, conflict, discrimination, ridicule, stress, and other potential obstacles to productivity and harmony. It sounds like an unrealistic job description. It can be done, and great pleasure can be derived from creating an environment where others find a rewarding work-life balance.

Who's The New Guy?

There was a time not so long ago when it was expected that you would spend most of your career working for the same organization. There were pension plans, retirement gold watches, and unrelenting loyalties to your employer, but those days passed us like horse and buggy. If your resume listed more than one or two prior establishments along your career path, then you were deemed by HR to be a risky hire in that you likely would only stay with the company for a few years or maybe even ten but certainly not worth the jeopardy of extending an offer in most cases. Today, the exact opposite is true. If you don't show a progression of career moves, you do not possess the necessary skills to be deemed promotable or attractive to a headhunter organization. Loyalty is a weakness in today's market and a black mark on your curriculum vitae (CV).

My career settled comfortably between the two extremes. When I began my management career, remaining within the same organization and building internal connections and skills to achieve promotion was favorable. Along the way, I learned of the looming change in philosophy. I moved to further my career by applying for posted opportunities and making connections that translated into recruitment opportunities for available positions. In every case, there were new beginnings within the same organization or with an entirely unfamiliar corporate structure. I was the "new guy" on many occasions, with a new job title in a new organization, location, or branch of my current employer.

Regardless of the circumstances, the scenario was nearly always constant. The existing employees were interested in discovering who I was and how I operated as a manager. The smaller details, such as marital status, children, prior career experience, vehicle type, likes and dislikes, etc., could be uncovered later. Still, they needed assurances that some egomaniac jerk hadn't been hired to deliver great distress to them all. Their primary concern was for themselves and how this change in leadership would directly or indirectly impact them. At this juncture, many options exist for the manager placed in this position. Some would start by holding court and delivering a sad message about how this ship would sail under their captaincy and how any mutineers would be addressed. A clear message that they were in charge and any insubordination would be responded to harshly and quickly. They will decide the proper procedures to move forward and aren't interested in the opinions or suggestions of the existing team. Ultimately, an "if you don't like it – there's the door" mentality.

Some other newly appointed leaders might be under-experienced enough to try and merely replace the exiting manager and allow the prior administration's daily activity to continue with an "if it's not broken – don't try to fix it" strategy. The trouble with this effort is blatantly obvious. Suppose the departing supervisor left of their own accord while the business was functioning well. In that case, the replacement leader has a challenge and must quickly prove their ability because any change will be reluctantly accepted. Any drop-off in performance will be noted soon and under extreme magnification. It's much more difficult to replace a well-liked leader leaving behind a team operating efficiently. Additionally, implemented revisions will be questioned about effectiveness and often rejected with comments, "Well, that's not how so and so would have done it." Alliances with a departing leader usually run very deep to those left behind when the operation ran favorably. Someone else's success is just that and really cannot be absorbed as your methodology. If you opt for inaction, your team will quickly realize that you bring very little to the table and will slowly marginalize your authority and operate as they always have, thus making any future attempts to initiate modification or adjustment difficult.

If the prior manager was terminated because of a policy violation or merely underperforming, then failure to introduce a sequence of alterations addressing the delinquencies signals that the new sheriff is just as corrupt as the old one. Moving forward without change is dangerous. Trying to allow the status quo to rule the roost is not one I would recommend. The methods in place were ineffective or violated operating standards and required an immediate realignment to expected procedures and policies. Being the "new guy" can be an easy transition or one that is quite difficult and requires straightforward actions designed to bring operations into acceptable and then exceptional performance of the team in place. Suppose the departing manager was well liked and admired by the team, and you establish yourself as ethical, straightforward and concerned for their success. In that case, before much time has passed, they will become your team and remember the prior manager fondly but without remorse because you are the new champion.

The approach that I found to be most effective for my administration was a strategy of non-interfering observation, distillation, and interpretation, and then manipulation. Upon introduction to the existing team, I would put them at ease with the assurance that I wasn't brought in merely to initiate radical change. I backed that up with the acknowledgment that some degree of modification to the existing team and performance model would most likely occur but to harbor no unfounded fear if they were performing as expected and to return to their everyday operations. I would follow the initial allaying of fear with an announcement that I would observe how things were executed routinely and, after consideration, either make changes directly or consult those performing the tasks to discover mutually agreed-upon modifications. These pronouncements usually set their minds somewhat at ease. Side note - It is usually the nails that stick out that get the attention of the hammer. As I was still the unknown, most adopted a "wait and see" attitude. Although some held beliefs of ulterior motives, most attempts to increase their effectiveness often served to ease their workload through greater efficiency. As the first week drew to a close, the needed adjustments were usually quite easy to notice, and the commencement of modification would begin. Unless the observed transgression or misconduct required immediate and radical adjustment because of flagrant policy violation or safety concerns, negligible, subtle behavioral changes were introduced. Just enough in most instances to begin to put your "stamp" upon the operation while still establishing that you acknowledge their existing efforts and successes, both prior and current. Assurances also that their legacy will only be enhanced with your guidance and not completely rebuilt because they were failing. Once this truth is accepted and the stress level of the change in leadership has subsided, additional, more drastic implementations can be undertaken where required. Before long, your team will look forward to your leadership and not backward upon what it once was.

There were situations where this approach would not have served me well. In my career, I have served in management for seven leading organizations, including two of the top three national pharmacy chains. One experience was very rewarding, and I enjoyed my tenure a great deal and, to this day, have nothing but favorable things to say about the organization. I cannot say that about the other. This organization operates in more than 2000 locations, and I can only attest to my experience in the early 1990s – maybe they have improved as years and additional acquisitions have transpired. I relate my experiences with the local stewardship. When I left their employment, I had not had the opportunity to interact with any representative beyond the regional level. The regional and district upper management was unprofessional, the policy violations were severe and frequent, and the working conditions were frightful. Suppose I hadn't been employed by some of the top professionally administered companies prior to my experience with this pharmacy outfit. In that case, I might not have noticed so many discrepancies in the treatment of their employees. I had a solid foundation of proper employee-facing policies and human relations, so this lack of professionalism was alarming.

While being in their employ as a store manager, I was utilized as what I would term a "hatchet man" by the powers that be. The upper management recognized my prior experience in operating some of the highest revenue-generating locations in the area while serving as general manager with their biggest rival competitor and instead of building upon those valuable skills, they assigned a miserable existence. They would relocate me to one of the lowest performing locations they operated with the request to "clean it up." Not only was the store underperforming, but the area in which it was located was rundown and dangerous, and the staff desperately needed meaningful training and leadership. I would arrive on day one and think, "What the hell has happened here?" The store would be in shambles, the shelves understocked, the floors filthy, windows either shuttered or so dirty you couldn't see through them anyway, and the team wandering with no clear leader. I would then interview the team to assess their knowledge and desire to remain in the employee group. I would subtly test and try to understand the knowledge and commitment of existing "assistants" if any such staff were also assigned there. I'd do an in-depth survey of the store to determine what was needed from an ordering perspective, what was on hand, what was overstocked, and what was being lost in reoccurring thefts. Loss prevention practices were non-existent and the suspicion and lack of trust was infused from the top leadership on down.

I would review maintenance needs, schedule their completion, and review banking and revenue paperwork from the past months or longer to uncover internal theft. The list was almost endless, and there was zero assistance from above. They didn't respond to questions or requests for advice or additional payroll dollars. All efforts had to be achieved using the budgeted dollars assigned to the location. However, I was free to spend as much of my time there as was required without additional compensation. There was a mandatory six-day work week, so working a seventh day or a series of six extended days was considered justified. Since my departure from the company, word of the regional operation failures found its way to the national level, and changes were made. I hope they were so appalled, thus prompting the dismissal of the regional leaders - believing they were terminated because the organization doesn't operate in that manner. I'd hope for such a change, but I do not know if that was the case. Is there any bitterness here?

Regardless, implementing change was immediate and drastic in situations such as this. There could be no soft approach if any true impact were to be had. In addition to reviewing and adjusting all the other items essential to a smooth-performing location in terms of appearance and stock on hand, I had to make personnel adjustments. Sadly, this nearly always involved the termination and replacement of most teams and, in a few cases, the entire staff. I would never say that I got "used" to firing employees because it has never been a pleasurable experience for me. Still, some circumstances eased the difficulty of discontinuing their employment by the existence of tangible proof of policy violation. This removed any "personal" ramifications and made it strictly a "business" transaction by their actions.

Upon successful implementation of these needed changes, the location would begin to perform up to acceptable expectations within two to six months after assuming control of the location. Shortly thereafter, I would be reassigned to another location with a legacy of disastrous performance to begin the process all over again. I continued this dreadful course for nearly two years until my son was born, and I could afford to pursue a career change without fear of a health insurance lapse during pregnancy. In that period, I brought this type of change to six locations, and with each subsequent reassignment, my first day was preceded by my newly acquired reputation as the "blood-letter" or "hatchet man." It's not exactly the moniker I aspired to be labeled as, but it fits the role they pigeonholed for me. Drastic change was inevitable in these poorly operating locations, and being preceded by this expectation of extensive staff turnover made it very easy to determine who was immediately on the chopping block. Those who had been underperforming or perhaps even committing criminal activity either jumped ship immediately or were relatively easy to spot as undesirable. They were sometimes revealed to me through one-off conversations with their peers. Honest employees take umbrage in some instances because they interpret the underhanded dealings of others as a direct affront to their honesty and integrity. Often, they protect the property and interests of the parent company as their own and defend it against disloyal teammates. You cannot train someone to carry these attributes as they are either naturally inherited or non-existent.

When you are successful in leading teams, a genuine sadness prevails when you are reassigned to another location, promoted, or merely opt for an opportunity elsewhere. The cohesive "family" you have created is temporarily lost in its familiarity and routine with your departure. Sometimes, your former team may attempt to retain the relationship through phone calls, emails, texts, or by dropping into your new location if possible. Of course, you experience loss as well, but you can counter it with the excitement of the unknown you are about to discover. They, however, are left with the unsettling unknowns again. The awkward discovery of the style, traits, and direction that will be instituted by the next "new guy." It is a distressful situation when circumstances bring you back to that location and you discover the standards have been allowed to falter and the team is suffering from the diminished leadership of your replacement. They might look to you for an answer to their new reality but unless you want to make an enemy of one of your peers, your hands are somewhat tied. A word in confidence to upper management may help alleviate some of the misery of your former "family".

Something magical develops as a phenomenon throughout your career. Members from many different organizations and locations of the larger companies you've been employed by as a manager form an extended "family" of sorts. It's wonderful that these folks have grown beyond the boss-subordinate relationships and truly consider themselves friends and intimates. I have a small group of friends I have been involved with since high school or college, and a few others have joined that rank through neighborhood introductions in the various areas where I have lived. Still, most of the "friends" I acknowledge have been culled from my work experiences. Granted, not all of these are as intimate as some life-long relationships, but they are enough to engage in relatively personal confidence. The relationship with these individuals is often permitted to blossom into something with deeper impact because the boss-employee relationship no longer exists, and the invisible line becomes just that – invisible and truer relationships can develop. My personal experience has been that after a 40-plus-year career, being the new person in charge can be exciting and extremely frightening at the same time.

When you have a clean slate when choosing a team while establishing a brand-new organization or a new location for an existing company during expansion, the challenges are quite different. The daunting task of remolding and upgrading someone else's staff is removed, and you will need only select, train, develop, and ultimately upgrade your team. Although somewhat easier to administer, there is never perfection. Short-term satisfaction can be obtained, but ultimately, people "go bad" for lack of a better phrase. Personal turmoil, sickness, death, perceived opportunities elsewhere, conflict with another employee, relationship issues, disagreement with the company's direction, or a policy, in particular, are just a few of the potential downfall items for your team members. It's foolish to believe that all your staff is always happy and fully vested with no thoughts or intentions of leaving your side. Regardless, the successful manager will recognize this fact, treat them with the respect and understanding they deserve as human beings, and develop the relationships I have described.

As leaders, we all encounter those under our supervision who are "perfect" in their roles and perform exactly as we instruct, guide, and develop because of our instruction or divine natural talents. Sometimes, it's a combination of those skills and a desire to succeed and to please us. Whatever the reason, we are somewhat enamored with these individuals and do our best to aid them in their quests for advancement. Often, with uncanny ability, they predetermine and initiate actions you hadn't quite established yet on your own "To Do" list. You find yourself in awe of what you observe and hopefully gracious enough to commend them on their forethought and ability to see the "big picture" before giving direction. Those special coworkers are rare and of extreme value to your team and the organization you represent. Inevitably, however, the day will come when, with a hat in hand, they will meekly submit their resignation letter. I say meekly because they will demonstrate remorse or contrition in leaving this home they have lived in comfortably and will most likely be on the verge of emotional, internal, and external turmoil. They will leave because they have completed whatever formal training program they have been pursuing, and its now time for their "real job," or they have been promoted within the organization to a higher position in a different location. Quite possibly, another business has spotted their exemplary work in your organization and wisely offered them a position they could not refuse.

Here's the difficult role for you as manager and mentor you must now assume – cheerleader. Regardless of how difficult it will be for you personally and professionally, you must put on your best face, congratulate them wholeheartedly, and celebrate their achievement. That is the only fitting and reward for their years of service to the team and to you in particular. If they have been promoted within the organization, you have succeeded in the leadership role to the best possible outcome. It's a feather in your cap and not a loss of an extremely valuable member of the team. Perhaps, one day, you'll be reporting to them as your supervisor. That would be the ultimate satisfaction of a successful leader. Regardless of the circumstance, sincerely wish them the utmost success in their new situation and assure them that you will always be there for them should they need advice (professional and personal), references, or even a decision to return to your employ should the grass not be as green on the other side of the fence as advertised. Like a proud parent, stand back and let them fly from the nest. Never burden them with any guilt trips about "How will I possibly replace you?" or "That company will chew you up and spit you out." The last thing you want to do is sour this relationship that has been so rewarding to your team and both of you personally. Man up and wave those pom-poms!

Do Unto Others

When I consider what a customer's experience should be when frequenting an establishment for a particular purpose, the answer always arrives at the same conclusion. To me, the customer should be treated as the sole purpose of that business. I always emphasized that concept to my teams. Treat customers as you wish to be treated by others when you are the client. So often, we experience an interaction where we are made to feel as if we are interrupting their work instead of being the reason behind it. As organizations grow and sales increase, team members are often expected to do additional tasks over and above their normal workload. Just as frequently, the staffing model is not adjusted to increase the number of coworkers on staff, or in some instances, they have been lessened in headcount.

Committed employees will most often take this added responsibility in stride and perform admirably with the proper recognition and reward. Frequently, when the dyke is about to burst, niceties usually go untendered by overwhelmed and overburdened managers. Instead, they dictate and demand the increased chores be performed without complaint and without addressing the underlying causes associated with this new dynamic. The result is a group of associates that begin to resent the escalated activity and expectation and, in turn, direct their anger and resentment toward the one person with no clue of the tension brewing just below the surface - the customer. Perception is reality in the realm of the customer, and an unprovoked attack from one of your employees is unexpected and certainly unwarranted. The customer has no idea that the employee is feeling overworked, stressed out, and somewhat bitter about the current conditions when their prior experiences recall contentment of your teammember. This can result in rude, unfriendly service exhibited by your team, which must be unacceptable under the standards you have established for them. So, what methods can you employ to ensure this doesn't occur?

A critical first step is acknowledging the change in direction and the reasoning behind it. Employees will frequently conceive of an "us against them" mentality about an organization's upper management, and it's your role to interpret the directives handed down to your teams. Your folks look to you for that explanation and help them to grasp the "why" behind the directive. You are usually afforded only one chance to do so before they begin to offer their distorted decoding of the perceived hidden agenda of the home office. When initiatives and policies are issued, and you are directed to implement them, it's important to seek understanding if you have any doubts or reservations as to the validity of the directives and get as much clarification as possible before the roll-out. You represent authority and command the leadership seat regarding counsel about the proposed institution of the upcoming change. You must walk the fence between representing the organization and being their leader and champion of their future well-being. It can be a difficult position to be placed in, particularly when the proposed modification requires an unpopular component. Yet, there you are.

You must portray the vested partner on both sides and initiate the alteration, making it palatable for all parties concerned. Addressing the honest concerns of your team members while relaying the benefits anticipated by the organization will allow you to remain objective and flexible to react with the needed responses to unanticipated issues that may arise. You must not publicly assume the attitude of "What on Earth are they thinking?" even if those are your thoughts privately.

Betrayal of the organizational leadership will undermine the objectives of long-term policy and practices in the eyes of your team and instill an environment where it is nearly impossible to wrangle them back into strict adherence to future directives. Casual comments should be avoided; only addressing legitimate concerns is important to maintaining your ability to manage them as a cohesive unit. If they believe you do not endorse the upper management, they will disparage them at every opportunity. It can be rather like getting your two-year-old to eat broccoli sometimes. It would help if you convinced them that even though they might not enjoy the experience, it is still important because.... I would never support any directive that would cause harm or endanger a team member's well-being.

Not surprisingly and understandably, most initiatives usually involve a perceived increase in workload. Acknowledging this purported expansion of duties is vital in assuring they will begin the process with the clear-cut understanding that at least someone in the organization appreciates their accelerated effort. At the minimum, they will exert a valid attempt at achievement to satisfy their respect and belief in you as their leader. Failure on your part to set up this situation will lead to dissatisfaction with you as well as those above your pay grade. It also falls to your responsibility to evaluate this new initiative. You must gauge its effectiveness after a short period, its impact on the team, and whether you should continue to endorse it or make suggestions for alterations to those higher up in the organization. It also rests with you to make immediate changes should any negative impact become overwhelmingly significant and dramatic shifts in behavior have been observed.

That brings us back to the impact these added tasks often present on customer service levels. The well-being of your customers equals the well-being of your team, and neither can be allowed to suffer without corrective steps being taken by the manager. When your previously attentive and pleasant teammate is suddenly treating your customer as an obstacle to getting their assigned workload complete, you must act to ensure that this doesn't happen again. By natural inclination, some of our teammates will always present an evenhanded and pleasing appearance to our customers. It's just what they do and how they naturally operate. The remainder has been well-trained by you to administer a top-notch similar service, and any negative deviation from this will become evident quickly. If you determine that the dramatic metamorphosis is directly related to the newly implemented program, you must find a solution to relieve pressure on your team.

Indifferent and inattentive staff members cannot be condoned and will adversely and indelibly impact your business to the detriment of future growth and success. The good news here, however, is that these team members who have strayed from the straight and narrow can quickly come back into the fold with the lessening or removal of the recently added requirement. If the program itself is repealed or revamped at the highest level, it is permissible to acknowledge the error and thank those on your team for exposing the potential damage. Think of the crime spree that engulfed the United States in the 1920's-1930's because of prohibition and the return to "normalcy" after its repeal in 1933. Overworked teams will become unproductive teams. Mistakes are increased, leading to additional stress levels, which beget additional errors, and the cycle becomes vicious.

One of my favorite expressions is "there is never enough time to do it right but always enough time to do it over." Pressure to perform tasks in a timeline or environment overtly outside the normal sets the stage for failure. The argument is inevitably one in which the perpetrator of the mistake will assert that they could not render a perfect product or service level because of inadequate time or materials available. Regardless, this inferior product or service cannot be presented to the end user, so the process must begin anew, and a perfect result is the only acceptable outcome. The adage applies that there wasn't enough time the first time, but now there is enough time to recreate the desired product or service. If they had just adjusted to the demands of the situation and assured their success in the initial effort, there would be no reason to revisit it. As the team manager, you must plug the leak in the boat and find the culprit causing the damage. Correct it, learn from it, submit feedback if necessary, and reinforce your team's belief in your commitment to their success.

As the manager of many locations and the varied business models of those organizations, I had the pleasure of being employed by, there were several adages I found to be constant. One such belief was to "under promise and over deliver." What I mean by this phrase is that in the interaction with customers or clients, it was important to me that those on my teams never assured a consumer that our organization or specific location would perform a service or provide a product we could not render in a timeframe impossible to meet. In this manner, we would never disappoint or displease one of them by not living up to our pledge. This is not to say that we were never presented with a situation where an unforeseen obstacle emerged, and we were either late or unable to perform our promised service or product. That did happen on more occasions than I care to remember, but it was caused by the nature of the businesses or particular circumstances and, thus, unavoidable.

Fortunately, the outcome that was much more frequent was the other side of the coin, where we over-delivered on the transaction. Maybe it was just the timeframe promised that was delivered sooner than expected or perhaps the ability to receive a product that was out of stock at the competitors that our favorite customer just "had to have." Oftentimes, the quality of the product received was well above and beyond their expectations thus elating them or perhaps enhancing their own organization's image. There were so many methods and experiences that some customers commented that they would never consider leaving our relationship for a less-expensive competitor or because of any bad-faith experience. Keeping a valued client happy is much easier than obtaining new customers. It requires nothing more than a reliable team with a belief in the organization's long-term success, and that environment can be created by only one person – you, the manager. Under promise – over deliver.

You set the example they will emulate and follow. If you are indifferent to your customers, they will be as well. If you walk past trash on the floor, they will never glance at it. If you bad-mouth the corporate structure and those in positions of authority, they will have no respect for them and attempt to break the rules or shun responsibilities. But if you notice the line at the cashier station has grown to three and the second cashier you have on duty is still at lunch. You operate a register to immediately alleviate the congestion and make your customer smile and your lone cashier sigh with relief, you have set the tone for everyone else. Is there anything more frustrating in today's marketplace than approaching the checkout station and realizing that you are about to queue up in an incredibly long line without the hope of a quick transaction? There are many stations, yet only a few are being manned, and even the emerging self-service cashier stations are either closed or overwhelmed. You can excuse this situation if you observe a manager attempting to adjust staffing to accommodate this increase in transactions and showing concern for your inconvenience. What you cannot excuse and are more frustrated by is the manager standing idly somewhere checking messages on their phone or talking to another staff member who is not concerned about the traffic backup at the cashier's stations. Your clients will also observe how you respond to situations and judge your worthiness for their business by the type of ethics you purport. This often goes beyond your team and customers in that your peers will recognize these traits and will usually learn their methodologies based on good and bad observations from their peers.

Don't Air Your Dirty Laundry

Upon entering a retail establishment recently, I was immediately thrust into a loud, ugly, heated conversation regarding a situation that the two employees present had found themselves dealing with. From what I could gather from the escalating accusations yelled back and forth, one of them had requested a particular day off. Now, the schedule has been modified without their prior knowledge or consent to accommodate the needs of the other employee present. Allegations of favoritism and sexual encounters flew between the two parties until one huffed away, and the other was left in tears. Neither gave any consideration nor attention to the customers in the store. Every aspect of their business decorum had broken down instantly, and no one was there to sew the torn fabric back together. As this was an establishment where food was served, my immediate instinct was to head directly back outside to my vehicle and drive away as fast as possible to another venue where an angry chef handling my soon-to-be-ingested ingredients was less likely to be at the stovetop.

I feel reasonably confident that most of my readers have encountered a similar situation. It's somewhat embarrassing to witness this internal turmoil. Certainly, it presents a dilemma as to whether to continue to frequent the business at that moment or perhaps in the future. The commentary doesn't require scandalous ridicule or accusation to present the same discomfort or perhaps mortification to the client. Casual conversations between staff members can be just as disquieting to the unsuspecting browser. Carelessly tossed about comments regarding other employees or management can be easily overheard by anyone and, although unintended, can present fodder for complaint, outright shock, or scandal. Discussions of upcoming promotions, planned expansion, or store closures, including potential layoffs, are bantered about without regard to their proprietary or confidential nature. Every organization has operational objectives and planned initiatives that require discretion and, in some cases, stealth until unveiled and any anticipated market innovation can be easily undone. The ship "sunk" by a few loose lips. Corporate spies and "shoppers" are visiting stores every day to gain insight into the competition and try to enhance their market share at the expense of their rivals.

As your business's manager, how do you prevent this from occurring in your establishment amongst your team? It just boils down to expectations set by you for them and modeled by you before them. My favorite definitions of "manager" are these (authors unknown): "Leadership is a function of knowing yourself, having a vision that is well communicated, building trust among colleagues, and taking effective action to realize your leadership potential." Also, "Leadership is setting an example worthy of being followed by others." You must establish trust in your team that the vision you present for them to emulate and adhere to is worthy of their respect and that the organization represented by you and through you, therefore, is genuinely deserving of that respect.

They must truly believe that it is in their utmost interest to perform to the standards as the reward will be fulfilling monetarily and emotionally. A belief that there is an inherent importance to the successful completion of their responsibilities as the only possible comprehensive, successful outcome. A tall order. It is, but it is also quite doable for the skilled manager. Set the stage with clear, concise expectations, never deviate from them, and correct any missteps as soon as they occur. Inspect what you expect. You will never know if your team abides by the required standards of conduct if your observations are from a remote office. Frequent and uninterrupted interaction within the team is the most impactful way to monitor behavior and make adjustments. Surprise visitation is a dynamic method of uncovering behaviors that are deviant from the norm under the pretense that what the boss doesn't know won't hurt him mentality. "When the cats are away, the mice will play" – you can bet your bottom dollar on that truth! Stop in at odd hours, make an unexpected phone call, or perhaps send a neighbor or a peer in for a spot check. You will be amazed at what you uncover.

Your team will be somewhat amazed at the knowledge you have gained remotely, and a reputation for having those eyes in the back of your head may soon be touted by your team. However, I do not encourage you to use the "I caught you" mindset. Open and direct communication with the offender and a reiteration of the expectations should produce a renewed allegiance within that team member, and they may, in turn, become one of your most trusted and valuable employees. You will have those precious employees that, regardless of whether no one is watching, will always perform at the same trusted level and, if caught by surprise, will have nothing to fear because they are as they should be.

The public airing of grievances will occur at some point in every organization. It is most often the result of one or a few members believing that they have been wronged or left out of a decision or event or just plainly snubbed by someone else in the workplace. Often, the object of their complaint or ridicule is a management team member or the manager. Frequently, the perceived injury has little or no merit, and a rehashing of the details will end the protestation. Other times, however, the employee will attempt to air this dirty laundry on the sales or production floor to elicit sympathy and justification for their grievance. This cannot be allowed to occur. Any overheard or reported conversations such as this must be dealt with immediately and sometimes severely.

Usurping the authority of the management team or the besmirchment of the reputation or professionalism of a member of it cannot be tolerated. To permit such a diatribe or criticism in private is ill-advised, but the act in public is reproachable. Immediate removal from the soapbox is advised, and a demand for explanation is warranted. During this interchange, all attempts should be made to defuse and derail any ill feelings held by the employee. Counsel a return to rationality and a resumption of their duties once assurances are made that there will be no recurrence of such outbursts, public or private. If their grievances are justified, a promise to correct the injustice should be made and acted upon to return their attitude to a full "go-team" cohesion and ensure their cooperation. Punishment for the offender, if warranted, must be doled out to the complainant's satisfaction, and peace and harmony must be restored. If the aggrieved will not agree to cease the public denouncements, they must remain removed from the public space either by re-assignment or suspension according to company policy. If no such policy exists, then an administrative leave is suggested while such a policy can be created to address the situation.

An open and democratic workplace is desirable and encouraged, but this behavior has no place in such a workplace. A chain of command and a grievance process must be adhered to when issues arise. Allowing the customer or client to become embroiled in the political entanglement of a few or a single disgruntled employee cannot be tolerated. Deliberate grandstanding or sudden emotional outbursts have the same impact on the innocent client, and your team must never publicly participate in these behaviors.

Water cooler gossip has been and most likely always will be a part of the modern workplace. Mostly, it's harmless discussions of last weekend's football game or who is peddling Girl Scout cookies this year. When the conversation deviates from around the cooler to the open forum in which outsiders and those uninvolved in the organizations' private operation are inadvertently immersed into the often-ugly banter or accusation, it must be prevented. Two clerks discussing the physical attributes of the new employee or the racially toned "joke" passed from shelf-stocking team members who think they are alone in the aisle are as potentially objectionable to the shopper as a personal affront. Any offensive or potentially upsetting conversations, whether implicit or explicit, have no place in the workplace, and a zero-tolerance policy is imperative. Schooling these teammates often and preemptively with reminders of their roles in company representation and the expected proper decorum is paramount. You may never prevent 100% of the occurrences. Still, with a solid game plan and frequent follow-up, you can tremendously impact how your organization is represented wherever you are in a leadership capacity.

Never Let Them See You Sweat

At this point, I feel another of what my children would call a "Dad's story" is in order. Cue the "dream sequence" special effects...

During my tenure as a manager, I've seen and experienced some unforgettable events. I've chased shoplifters through neighborhoods, initiated police interventions regarding persons exposing themselves in public; robbery suspects holed up in my outside trash receptacles apprehended by vicious K-9 dogs, parking lot accident victims treated, windows smashed by social protestors, windows shot out by rival gang activity, customer fist-fights, customer threats against employees (one episode being 100% imagined by the employee - that would make a book on its own), and a myriad of incidents involving bodily fluids of one type or another. Most I'd rather forget, and some I cannot erase.

In the atmosphere of a fast-food restaurant, a working manager sees and hears many things that sometimes are quite unusual and often unforgettable. One such event transpired on a normal Tuesday afternoon that transformed the lives of several people involved and had an indelible impact on the reputation of that branch of the leading fast-food chain itself. Anyone employed by a large corporation operating in many locations is aware of the practice of updating store layout and thus, the standard operating procedures that govern that floorplan. The same is true in the restaurant business. The operating procedures used in this location were ones in which a "holding bin" was employed into which all assembled sandwiches would be placed pending sale to potential consumers. There were very strict standards as to the length of time any certain item could be held before requiring it be discarded in the trash. In this manner, the freshness of the product was always assured, as was the ability to service customers quickly and with a hot, delicious product. When business slowed down between breakfast and lunch or lunch and dinner rushes, a crewmember would be assigned to monitor the holding bin and keep minimal stock on hand to assure service and minimize waste. However, when the "rushes" occurred, one of the managers on duty was usually assigned to assume control of food production. This particular style of the bin was open on the front for crewmembers to be able to grab items quickly, and it was also open on the rear-facing section so that newly prepared sandwiches would be added from that direction, thus guaranteeing that a "first in, first out" methodology always was in use. Furthermore, the bin was slanted slightly toward the front, so gravity would always move the older product toward the front to ensure it was taken next when someone ordered it.

The person "calling the bin" would direct the kitchen staff to produce sandwiches in specific amounts by calling for a run such as a "3 pull," "6 turns," or "12 sear" on regular (10:1 patties – 10 patties per pound of beef). This was standardized and ingrained in the kitchen crewmembers so well that there could be no misunderstanding about what was being asked for. For example, when asked for a "6 turn" run of hamburgers, the crewmember would place six patties in a straight line above the known hot spot on the grill top and set the timer. At the set interval, the timer would say it was time to "sear" the patties. The timer was reset, and the searing was complete. The next timer alert was to turn the patties over (this was before the "clamshell" type grills now used where both sides cook simultaneously). The cook would flip the patties (2 at a time) and re-set the timer. Since a "6 turn" had been requested, at this time, a fresh run of 6 patties was placed upon a different spot on the grill top, and a new timer was set, thus beginning the new cooking time. This pace could be continued until the bin caller was satisfied with food levels or, if not, then increased to a "12 turn" or "6 then 12 turn" or a "6 pull" (beginning the new run when the completed patties were pulled off instead of at the turn). In extremely busy periods, the next run could be initiated at the "sear" timer, thus speeding the delivery of fresh products even faster. It was not uncommon to have 36 to 48 patties in stages of cooking at any given moment. At the lowest production level, a "1 pull" would require one new burger patty to be placed onto the grill when the last completed patty was removed. The system was beautiful.

The same was used to produce every sandwich including the larger patties, fish options, and apple and cherry pies. A passionate commitment to exacting training methodology, tried and true SOP standards, and "Aces in their places" allowed this business juggernaut to capture the lion's share of the international marketplace. Jeff Bezos learned it here as a Miami teenager in the 1980s and look where it took him (190 billion and growing). As the crewmember performed these tasks, others were toasting and dressing buns to accommodate the fresh patties. It all ran smoothly and efficiently. The team members would continue in this fashion until the business slowed down again, and control of the holding bin could become less concerning while cleaning up the kitchen, front counter, and lobby areas took priority. Now that you hopefully can visualize the madness of a lunch rush, allow me now to get on with my story.

The lunch rush was in full swing, and an assistant manager was standing behind the bin and "calling" food production in the kitchen area. For the sake of our story, let's give alias names to those involved. Dan, our manager, was diligently trying to keep the food levels in the bin at levels that allowed for quick service for both the front counter staff and those working in the drive-thru area of the store. The ability to keep the drive-thru running smoothly and quickly was even more important than the service offered within the location at the front counter. Customers who were required to wait an additional minute or two for special order items (no onion or pickle, etc.) could merely stand off to the side or have their missing item delivered to their seat by a crewmember as soon as it was completed.

Drive-thru customers, however, presented an entirely different consideration. Any delay or error could cause a backup at the pick-up window, the payment window, the order speaker (single lane in those days), or the line stretching out into the street. The goal of every manager in our location was to put our "aces in their places," thus assuring great service at all times. So here we were on this Tuesday with Dan, making sure the drive-thru team could offer spectacular service, and the team consisted of an ace on the order-taking window, another ace on the pick-up window, and Steve (an ace only when his mood was right) the teammember assembling the order. Today wasn't his best day.

Our location was centered in the upscale neighborhood of town where most families were so affluent that their children only held summer jobs to buy gas for their new Porsche that mommy and daddy just bought them (a slight exaggeration). Most crew members were wonderful, and their attitudes at the front door were checked. The same could not be said for Steve consistently. On occasion, he would become a sarcastic, smart-mouthed, narcissistic, bullying pain in the ass. He was in the process of performance counseling and discipline but hadn't done enough to get himself fired. So, on this day, Steve was "running" for the drive-thru. Simply put, he noted the required items for the current order listed on the TV monitor posted in the drive-thru and assembled those items into a bag(s) to complement any soft drinks assembled for the order by the pick-up window crewmember. The order was handed out the window to the waiting customer, and off they went. The entire process from speaker to departure was supposed to be less than a minute or two (a well-running location would serve their customer in 25 seconds). Those orders where food was unavailable or delayed because of special orders had to be "parked" in specially designated spots, and having to take an order outside after completion was a disruption to the overall flow of the operation; thus, keeping food ready and team members hustling, it could be avoided most times.

What does this have to do with Steve? Yes, yes, I'm getting there. I don't quite know what thought processes were occurring in his head. Still, for whatever reason, Steve decided he would make a sarcastic remark directed at Dan every time he reached into or walked past the bin in completion of his prescribed order fulfillment. Dan was the only person within listening range of Steve's cutting remarks, so no one else knew of the tension building. Dan made several verbal attempts to convince Steve to stop his harassment, but to no avail.

When the steaming hot, fresh burgers are brought to the bin, the person calling the bin continues in their forward-looking position (monitoring business trends) and carefully wraps the individual items in their designated paper wrappers – one for plain hamburgers and the other for cheeseburgers – then slides them into their respective locations in the warming cabinet. As Dan is wrapping these fresh sandwiches, Steve passes by and makes what can only be described as the insult that was the "straw that broke the camel's back." Dan hurls the freshly wrapped sandwich he holds toward Steve without any rational thought or restraint. Pause here if you will. This action by the manager is 100% unacceptable and reprehensible. This is what I meant by the chapter title of never letting them see you sweat.

There can never be a time or occurrence that overwhelms you to the point of losing your composure and ability to continue your role as the supervisor or manager. The leader who is always poised and under self-control. The person they turn to when overwhelmed by the circumstances or events and absolutely must have your guidance in these darkest hours. That is who you must be. The rock. The "go-to" guy. Solid, unshakeable, and ready to enter that phone booth and change your clothes into an outfit complimented by a terrific little cape and maybe a pair of nifty tights. Simply put, you can't lose your cool. You must never allow the actions of an employee to force you into making what is ultimately the wrong decision.

This story certainly represents an example of exactly what I was writing about. What's that? What happened afterward? Wait, the story gets even more disturbing. When our buddy Steve ducked to avoid the incoming bombshell sent hurling his way by Dan, the missile continued in its trajectory. It flew unobstructed across the stainless-steel front counter and struck a woman customer squarely in the throat area. Here she was, standing unsuspectingly before the counter awaiting delivery of her just-ordered meal. From her perspective, everything is operating normally behind the counter when suddenly, she is hit full force by the now unwrapping hamburger. As it smashed into her throat, it virtually exploded - unleashing extremely hot juices, meat fragments, and, most dramatically, onion pieces that caused burns and traumatic shock. It wasn't what she was expecting from "fast food."

In the wake of this fiasco, Dan was immediately let go due to his role in the event. Steve, however, had to be retained on the team until HR was satisfied that enough documentation had been assembled against him and that he could be dismissed with no chance of a wrongful termination suit being brought against the company. As for the unfortunate woman who was injured in the burger bombing, I'll let you formulate your own ideas, but suffice it to say that misfortune can sometimes result in "fortune"-ate. She most likely was a turtleneck wearer afterward.

After all these years, I can look back on this event and laugh a bit, but certainly, at the time, it was no laughing matter, and the seriousness and gravity of the situation had to be blatantly stressed to the team. With the majority of them being so young and inexperienced, an event such as this had the potential to shape their outlook on many things for the rest of their lives. As a manager at the time, it was a clear duty and responsibility to ensure that those lessons were learned.

I'm reminded of another situation (oh, Dad, not another story!) that occurred at the same restaurant that summer. A customer had returned a cheeseburger to the front counter, stating it was too rare for their liking. As all burgers went through the same cooking protocol, it was natural to have a little pink meat and bloody juices on fresh burgers, but the cashier did as was instructed. She apologized and told the person in the kitchen to allow one to cook a little longer in replacement. She assured the customer she would bring the completed order to where they were sitting as soon as possible. She then took the burger, now missing a bite, that the customer had returned, wrapped it in its paper wrapper, and placed on top of the bin. The person calling the bin was distracted and didn't retrieve it immediately to dispose of it in the" waste" can. All waste was recorded and tabulated daily to provide critical business data and "yields" of certain products. A larger than normal waste amount was a strong indicator of poor production or "bin" calling and necessitating additional training. The person running for the drive-thru (thankfully, not Steve) thought it was the special-order burger for his customer and bagged it along with the remainder of the order, and thus, it was handed out the window. The angry customer stormed into the location, demanding to see the "manager."

The customer stated, "I ordered a cheeseburger without onions, and I got this burger with a bite taken out!" Before I could say anything, the crew member who had sat the burger atop the bin was nearby, heard the interaction, put two and two together, and quipped, "What are you complaining about? There are still three good bites left!" I am a person who enjoys a good joke and will trade barbs with anyone in good jest. To say it was hard not to laugh when I heard this remark is a huge understatement. I could not laugh, of course. The customer's ire turned toward the employee, and I shot them a look that said in no uncertain terms – "get out of here now!" In short order, I was able to explain things to the customers, calm them, and ultimately satisfy them. It was amazing how much a free meal can calm even the angriest person. The conversation with that particular team member afterward was stern yet occasionally lighthearted as I had to appreciate the audacity of what was said. It required a balanced lesson for the employee regarding personal security and the potential outcomes when dealing with outraged individuals. I tried but faltered to contain my enjoyment at the sheer amusement of what was said. The conversation might have been much more dramatic if the person involved had not been such a stellar employee before this mistake. Regardless, the event was documented in the file, and all promised future discipline was noted if a similar transgression occurred. Although I didn't keep my "manager face" throughout the incident (I may have even broken my mantra), it stands as one of the oddest and most memorable moments of my career.

Bits and Bobs

In this chapter, I'll look at some additional attributes, ideas, ideals, and suggestions that ended up on the cutting room floor (as they say) when I wrote the earlier chapters. They are just as noteworthy and perhaps of greater importance, yet they just didn't "fit" in the cohesiveness of those statements.

Traits that are desirable to seek, encourage, and nurture. I've discussed the positive and negative experiences I encountered working with so many individuals and teams throughout the years. The extensive list extolls the characteristics of the "ideal" employee, but these additional items cannot be overlooked.

A positive attitude. Is there anything more welcoming in the workplace than being greeted by a member of your team who is just oozing enthusiasm and desire to "hitch the horses" and begin another day of pleasurable and productive activity? Bringing that same passion day after day sets these individuals apart from everyone else and they are a treasure to any staff.

Situational empathy is another somewhat rare skill. To be able to listen to someone's complaint or expressed need is one thing, but to respond in such a way as to make their concern your own is another. These special folks possess a genuine kindness cherished by those they come in contact with. Most times, this skill requires active listening. There is a dramatic difference between hearing what someone is saying and listening to what they said, thus gaining understanding. Nothing could be more evident in this distinction than to pause in today's world and notice the constant stream of information zooming past your senses from all directions. You hear (or see) it all, but how much of it do you process and digest, truly feeding your understanding and knowledge? My guess is it's not very much. Who could latch onto everything? Engaging another human in one-on-one conversation requires both parties to commit to an uninterrupted and undistracted exchange of ideas or information.

When one of the parties allows for diversion from the contract, active listening becomes a casualty of inattentiveness, and the true, intended message is lost. The successful leader can tune into the transmission and accurately receive the intimated concept. It's genuinely listening to understand rather than listening to merely respond. The directives and instructions you bring to your team should congeal into a system of open-minded management. They should believe they are valued, esteemed, respected, and freely encouraged to offer ideas and solutions that will be considered and implemented if mutually agreed upon, collectively taking the approach which will be the best step forward. A cohesive team will consist of members who never need to apologize for their ideas. When you accomplish this ideal, your team will be unstoppable in its successes.

Undesirable Traits that need to be addressed metamorphosed into positive attributes or eliminated. There will be those you cannot convince or persuade into believing their methods or performance requires alteration. When this occurs, the best course of action is to re-assign their duties to alleviate the conflict or, as we used to say, "promote them to customers." Clashes of management style are natural and help build a stronger, more diverse workplace, but the characteristics I will address only tear at the fabric of good leadership. Sadly, the list is extensive. We discussed the ability to be genuine, and the lack of empathy is a cause for concern. The demonstration of truly not caring is abysmal and is now so commonplace that we begin to accept it as the norm. Negativity, whining, failure to give the best effort all the time, or displaying a "bothered" attitude will be tell-tale signs that this employee will soon cause turmoil within the ranks. This is the beginning of future failure to complete work assignments, dereliction of responsibility for their actions, and perhaps disrespectful or abusive behavior, becoming unresponsive to coaching or feedback. What follows are unexcused absences, misuse of company time, and uncooperative, oppressive, or provocative behavior resulting in poor job performance. The longer this decline in performance is allowed to fester, the greater the violations will occur. Employee theft, lying, absconding responsibility, perpetuating micro-aggressions, sabotage, threatening aggressiveness, unprofessional conduct while communicating with fellow teammates or customers, and often the inappropriate use of equipment or supplies, to name a few.

But why stop there? Let's explore many more thorns usually hidden from view on the newly picked rose we just introduced to our team. These cancerous growths unleashed are now being uncovered, to our surprise and dismay. They don't work well with others. They are resistant to change. They possess a certain arrogance (narcissism), have ineffective communication skills, or have professed skills that don't match the job responsibilities. They demonstrate inappropriate classroom or meeting behavior, such as yelling, talking over or interrupting others, monopolizing talks, or making unreasonable demands. There is a certain amount of jealousy of superiority in terms of rank. Pessimism, procrastination, disorganization, never taking ownership while not following through on assignments, and regularly making excuses for failures. A passive reluctance to respond or long delays in response to requested information or commitments signal a dismissiveness that cannot be ignored. Situational apathy, lazy listening, constant interrupting, and unreasonable or excessive demands on a leader's time, space, or attention are all forms of workplace bullying growing bolder. The seriousness of the violations continues to escalate, morphing into acts of arriving late and leaving early without consent, talking or spreading rumors about a person's personal life, distancing themselves from their other teammates, and maybe even workplace violence, resulting perhaps in sexual and/or physical abuse.

Removing the negative interactions this individual has with clients and crew members alike is paramount to retaining a safe and enjoyable work environment. Any hesitation by the management creates the potential for many destructive circumstances. The impact on co-worker morale, customer satisfaction, and business operations could be felt instantly, shortly, or perhaps leave a much deeper and longer-lasting scar. In this litigious society in which we find ourselves today, any perceived "chink" in the armor or believed failure on behalf of an organization opens it up for untold litigation and expense. Damages, both monetary and reputational, can skyrocket. As the guardian of the company's assets at the local level, it is your responsibility to monitor and act upon any perceived delinquency in the operation that could harm any party within the organization or outside (customers and vendors). Failure to do so can be disastrous to the organization and you personally if deemed responsible for the negligence.

We have explored the traits and indicators that a team member has fallen out of sorts and needs retraining or termination. Likewise, there are signals that your work environment has become toxic and needs attention. An astute leader can quickly recognize these warning signs and take the necessary steps to prevent further decay of the desirable operation standards. Some indicators may slowly creep in almost unnoticed, and others will be glaring. Regardless of the intrusion, once the flag has been raised, the dedicated leader will acknowledge the situation and address it immediately to ensure little or no damage to the business's reputation or the well-being of clients and co-workers alike. If you always talk on your cell phone or fail to provide adequate, constructive feedback, you have slipped on the blinders of mediocrity and deserve your upcoming consequences.

Creeping diseases include low morale, unproductivity, workplace stress, team member burnout, poor work-life balance, and high turnover - struggling to retain its best-performing employees - resulting in overtaxed, exploited workers and allowing these dysfunctional deficiencies to remain unaddressed leads to greater consequences and the impact felt by your customer base. Clients attempting to contact the managerial team frequently wait on hold for too long, are frustrated with poor automated phone prompts, are transferred multiple times, and are passed to various agents and touchpoints without satisfactory resolution. Managers who repeatedly prioritize rigid company policy above the customer needs while failing to assess the quality of customer service and ignoring customer feedback will probably wonder in amazement why the revenue has taken a nosedive. None are so blind as those that will not see. When customers can't reach you, and you fail to offer them (or your team) real-time support, you end up lying to employees and clients alike to keep the plates spinning in the air.

At the same time, you search for an exit strategy to this mess you've allowed to take hold within the operation you have been chosen to safeguard. Soon, long wait times combined with negligence in manufacturing will result in mistakes, waste, and unhappy customers. Errors and excuses will run rampant - escalating to greater and greater degrees of catastrophe. What's next? Overbilling of clients either accidentally or intentionally, compromising the customer's privacy, or, worst of all, the inability to post reliable hours of operation on your front door! We've all seen it and been impacted by it since the pandemic. Formerly reliable businesses post handwritten signs on their front doors, sadly announcing their incapacity to guarantee when their services will be available. Unfortunately, they may be "forced" to close earlier or open later than their normal hours of operation. They usually blame it on poor staffing or inability to hire. I say that is bull****. A seasoned and proactive leader is always prepared for the worst-case scenario. Yes, I had difficulty sourcing, recruiting, and hiring during the pandemic, but I never allowed it to impact my customers adversely. My team put in tremendous effort to get us through those trying days, but we did it collectively, and when it was becoming less severe, we celebrated as one team.

Ultimately, when dark storm clouds gather on the horizon and the winds of adversity threaten to tear the roof off the building and the windows rattle in their frames, you are the lifeboat, the anchor in the storm. Whether metaphorically speaking or meteorologically reality, above all else, you - as leader - absolutely must arise to the challenge and hold your team together and keep that boat from floundering. If you're like me, the larger the sea swell, the greater the thrill!

Wrapping up

In summary of the threads of thought and opinions rendered in prior chapters, I feel it's fitting and appropriate to offer up some sobering statistics in support. As a manager, leader, or supervisor – whatever title you find most suitable- you have the utmost responsibility to your subordinates, company stakeholders, and client base to monitor and maintain solidly principled and well-practiced business acumen. The numbers tell the truth. The damage inflicted upon a good team by a poorly trained leader or a manager who doesn't care or employs unethical methods can be devastating and possibly impossible to remedy and heal. If you refuse to be a "Good Boss" or don't wish to exert much effort to ensure success, find your new career working alone in some mundane production line or subject yourself to someone else's leadership who will bring a true passion to the role. You can point at me and say, "Yes, but you never made it to the top, did you?" That is true. I settled comfortably on the rung to which I ascended and wished to climb no higher. I peeked at the upper echelon and had no desire to model myself in that image. I could never be the cold-hearted, "all business" ass that walked over the broken backs and discarded bodies of others to get to the top. It just isn't in my nature. What was in my nature has been spelled out in these pages, and I've been rewarded with life-long friendships and the respect of those I've had the luxury of being associated with. As for me, I loved every minute of it!

Terry

<u>**Customer turnover.**</u>

(Source: Linnworks)

"In the United States, 80 percent will walk away after a couple of bad experiences even when customers love your brand. The challenge is that customers usually won't tell you they're unhappy. Only 1 in 26 disappointed customers complain. The rest leave."

(Source: Reputation Refinery)

- According to word-of-mouth marketing statistics, 96% of unhappy customers don't complain to the company about a bad experience; however, they share their bad experience with about 9-15 people.

- About 13% of unhappy customers share their bad experiences with 20 people.

- A happy customer, on the other hand, only tells <u>three people</u> about it.
- 91% of unhappy customers will not buy from a company they've had a bad experience with again.

- It takes about <u>40</u> positive customer experiences to undo the damage done by one negative review.

<u>**Team member turnover.**</u>

(Source: Indeed)

Top 16 Reasons Why Employees Choose to Leave Their Jobs

1. *Needing more of a challenge*

2. *Looking for a higher salary*

3. *Feeling uninspired*

4. *Wanting to feel valued*

5. Seeking a better management relationship

6. Searching for job growth and career advancement

7. Needing more feedback or structure

8. Wanting a different work environment

9. Looking to live somewhere else

10. Feeling conflicted with workplace policies

11. Thinking that their job has changed

12. Wanting a clearer company vision

13. Needing a better work-life balance

14. Seeking a more financially secure company

15. Wanting more independence

16. Looking for more recognition

From Those On The Team(S)

As I deliberated over what topics and what examples to include in this volume, I decided to reach out to several of the many former team members and peers that I had the pleasure of collaborating with during my career and inquire if they would be interested or willing to read this for critique and to offer a short "blurb" on their experiences with me as a leader or peer or friend. I was delighted with the overwhelmingly positive response from most of them. There were two who opted to "pass" on the request for reasons unknown despite a continued relationship with them through the years, so I can only assume they have nothing negative to add but elected to decline. What follows (in no particular order of importance) is a collection of those shared memories and encouragements. My undying love and respect for these important people in my life and the true reasons for any successes I experienced.

Terry Werner is not only a remarkable manager but also a close friend. He taught me valuable lessons about leadership that I will always cherish. Terry's approach to management was both friendly and productive, and he believed that making mistakes was a natural part of learning. He was fair and direct with his team, providing clear expectations that were easy to understand. He knew when to put the manager hat on and when to take it off so he could be a part of the team. Terry was always reliable, and we could count on him to provide the support we needed. Most managers will say they have an open-door policy, but with Terry, this was true. His door was always open to anyone.

Thanks to Terry's guidance, I succeeded in my management role for 18 years, always using the techniques he showed me. His leadership style made for a pleasant and productive environment. Terry was a fantastic role model; his kindness and determination inspired us all. He was always there for me when I needed him, and I can't thank him enough for allowing me to pursue my career. Terry will always be

remembered as someone who made a big difference in my
life and career. — Jennifer B.

Among all the varied and diverse personalities I encountered
in Specialty Retail Management, Terry Werner emerged as
more than just a leader but a guiding force in my
development and that of numerous other Managers. From
the onset, Terry described his strategic focus of aligning
with the company's core values and executing for results.
"Identify and align" is how I paraphrase now one of my first
lessons from Terry. This proved to be a roadmap to my
success.

Terry was more than a Manager; he was a mentor who saw
potential and actively nurtured it to fruition. He stressed the
importance of seizing opportunities as they presented
themselves, and I took this to heart. Under his watchful eye,
I navigated the retail landscape and made my way up the
ranks, leaning on Terry countless times for his unwavering
support as I enjoyed the success of my hard work. In the
process, I greatly improved my social skills and eliminated
previously existing barriers while forging and maintaining
bonds with my peers and partners. Terry's sage advice was a
constant for me in this evolving landscape.

Ultimately, I found in Terry not just a leader and mentor but
a friend whose driving force shaped my career and my
leadership approach. His advice and investment in me
proved to be invaluable. My success, and that of other
fortunate individuals like myself, is a testament to the
impact of a true Leader in Retail Management. — Gregg H.

I was honored when asked to say a few words about a man
who, regardless of the miles between us, I will always call
my friend.

Terry was the kind of manager who treated everyone with
respect and always welcomed his fellow workers' input on
making the workplace enjoyable AND productive.

A shining example of a forward thinker. Terry LIVED outside the box! I fondly remember phrases like, "Barry, I've got this great idea to share with you. What do you think??" He always comes up with ways to make his co-workers feel appreciated regardless of their position. No one is better than Terry in gathering and consolidating feedback into best practices.
A man who helped and supported me throughout my career. He is an inspiration to all who had the honor and pleasure to work with him!

When Terry talked... you WANTED to listen! Can you say that about your boss?? — Barry H.

Terry was my manager when I was promoted to assistant manager. Terry was my example of Management listening well, keeping the leadership team informed and supported, keeping the whole team motivated and working together, and holding people accountable without making work decisions personally. I still quote many things Terry taught me almost 15 years ago, especially to myself, to keep my feet on solid ground. Most recently, the concept of 'management by walking around' (maintaining awareness, positive interaction, accountability, correction). — David S.

In the spring of 2009, I worked for Terry as a courier for X. I had the happy circumstance of driving from Indianapolis to Dayton, Ohio, to pick up materials printed at a centralized printing facility and return those jobs to Indianapolis for distribution. I started at 5:00 am and ended at 1:00 pm. It was my dream job because I have always loved driving, especially long distances. If you've ever had a job you looked forward to attending every day, you know how I felt. I LOVED that job. But then I was informed my life would get a lot better...I was to become a grandfather.

Sasha was born, and I was more captivated than I was as a parent. My wife and I became her sole babysitter from morning through evening, and over the next four years, Sasha and I were inseparable.

My days were awesome... drove to Dayton, returned to Indianapolis, and played with my grandchild for the rest of the day. Every day. Unfortunately, as things sometimes happen, the hammer fell: my daughter-in-law was promoted to Assistant Vice President at her mortgage company, which led to a reassignment to Arizona.

I was heartbroken. Devastated. You may as well have taken my child from my arms. Except this was worse.

Arizona is a long way from Indiana, especially when you don't have the money to jump on a plane whenever you feel like it. My wife and I made plans to visit, but medical reasons forced us to drive, which would take about three days each way, and company policy limited us to one week off at a time, even if we saved more vacation. I had a dilemma, as well as a broken heart. Six months of endless tears they led to Terry calling me into his office to ask what he could do.

I thought he'd laugh when I asked for July (the entire month) as a vacation, but he didn't bat an eye, raise an eyebrow, or place his hand over his mouth. Terry said, "Yes, of course. I'll make it work, Jim, don't worry about a thing. Consider it done, and if you need anything else from me, say the word." I couldn't believe it. I don't know how he sold this to the District Manager, but he did. I don't know how he sold it to my coworkers, but he did. This time off affected not only the couriers and Offices (and customers) in Indianapolis but also involved X workers in Ohio, far outside our district in Indiana. But true to his word, Terry made it happen.

Now, the months and years roll by, and I've retired and happily moved to Arizona (of course I did; what did you expect?), where, once again, I have the pleasure of playing with, teaching, coaching, and helping guide my grandchild's life.

But that summer will be one I won't ever forget, and nor will I forget the kindness shown to me by Terry Werner. Kindness, made more profound because he didn't have to do it. He willingly bent the rules for one of the least important employees in the system. Terry, I will always be grateful for that and for showing me what leadership can do when people care about one another. It may not have been that much for you, Terry, but it was huge to me, my wife, and my granddaughter. I'll never forget. — Jim S.

Working with Terry was a great experience. The first thing that stuck out about Terry's management style was his ability to maintain his cool despite adversity. Terry never seemed bothered. He stayed calm, so in turn, it kept the team calm. We often had deadlines that were sometimes unreachable, but Terry was about getting it done to the best of our ability, and more often than not, we got it done on time! I remember one Christmas, Terry gave me a gift - he may not have realized it, but that gift forever changed me in the best way possible. It's wild when I think about it. Even though Terry gave everyone the same thing, I remember thinking it must be nice to receive a gift from the manager. I never thought he thought enough of me to give me a gift, as I had never received one from my previous managers. When he gave me mine, I took it so personally. I felt like he thought enough of me to provide me with something more than words. With this, he showed me. The effects of Terry giving me led me down a path of giving all my future associates gifts depending on the various holidays they celebrated. Good associates and challenged associates alike; every associate working with me with a child in my family gave something even more substantial, all because of that gift Terry gave me. I remembered that feeling and loved seeing that look on various associates' faces. Thank you, Terry, for showing me being Calm & a little human with coworkers/associates can go a long way. That was more than 17 years ago when I had the pleasure to work with/ Terry Werner. I could say so much more about Terry's influence on me in the short few years I was in his presence. Thanks, Terry. — Robert (Carolinahblu) H.

Terry can bring out the best in people. His passion for mentoring and teaching gives him the right amount of patience to deal with tough situations and enough pressure to push those on the fence into action. And he wasn't afraid to roll up his sleeves and work alongside us when the busy season arrived.

Through his guidance, I found myself in leadership and led a successful team for many years. Today, I still find myself using some of his concepts regarding time management.

The time management concept that I speak of is that of the boulders (big projects that you have to chip away at over time), the large rocks that go in between, then the smaller ones that you can knock out one after another, and the sands of daily tasks that you do In between. You described that to me once differently, but it has always stuck with me and works! — Angela C.

I started working for Terry when I first moved to Indiana and had just graduated college. I felt very fortunate for the opportunity to receive mentoring from him at such a crucial time in my career. Terry is a wise and patient manager, as I witnessed this by the amount of time he took to teach me about retail and customer service. Terry always made me feel empowered and gave me communication techniques that I still use in my current job in healthcare. He always encouraged us to learn new techniques and different aspects of customer service. Terry always encouraged me to continue my education and had an open-door policy. My favorite thing about Terry was his pride in doing a great job and being an excellent manager. I could've seen myself working for Terry for a long time if I didn't have a dream of becoming a nurse. — Morgan G.

What do you expect out of your first big girl job? A big paycheck? This allows you to do all the things you could never do when working at minimum wage. A new car? Gone will be the times of check engine lights and rumbling motors. Security? Knowing that you've made it to a stable place, you can start building on it. Of everything you thought you'd get, a mentor was never on the list.

When I first started at xxxxxxx, I had big aspirations about where it would take me. Maybe a corner office, maybe an executive suite? It took me to downtown Indianapolis. Which, I know, doesn't sound too exciting. But being down there, in the thick of it, sometimes felt like I was the star of my own dark sitcom. No laugh tracks here. Just a lot of "How can I help you?", "My pleasure." and "Have a great day!".

It wasn't all so bad. After my first big promotion, I moved to the store that was in the heart of the city. With it, I gained a boss whom you could also call the heart of the city. Terry Werner.

Terry gave me a chance when no one else would. He saw how much I wanted to move up and how good I was at my job, and he gave me a shot. A shot I will always appreciate. He never expected me to know what I didn't know. If there was any skill, task, or ask I didn't know how to do, he was always willing to teach me. I never had to worry that things would go wrong as long as Terry was in the building.

With that also came trust. Terry trusted me to do my job and do it right. And when the chips were down, he never made me feel inferior or talked down to. Which is a skill most managers or bosses are lost on. Terry trusted that the team and I would do the right thing. And we did for him.

Terry was more than a boss, sure. Work was a priority; we all had bills to pay, but he made sure to make the place feel as welcoming as possible. It's really easy to turn a customer service position into a horrific dystopia. There were days when a lot of us wanted to call it quits. But never because of Terry. He was the reason we stayed.

The world changed a lot in 2020. The sure thing we all once counted on was up in the air, and who knows when it would come back down.

Riots in the streets, anger in their hearts. But who can blame them? And then comes the cleanup.

The store was in shambles. Little did we all know Terry's undeniable work ethic would put him in a position that would make it so he couldn't come back to us (work injury).

Whether it was divine intervention or just a crazy random happenstance, the events of late 2019 through mid-2020 changed everything. But I wouldn't have changed meeting Terry for the world. — Kassie G.

I was one of 3 profitable stores that reported to Terry. The business model was geographically based on stores. All sizes, large, medium, and small stores fed into your main hub location. You were our group manager, and it was such a great time. You provide a balance between work, life, and friendship support. You gave me all the support as a manager I could have ever hoped for. We worked really well and hard as a group of 4 stores collaborating together. As my direct manager, Terry took the stress of corporate away from us, which was a great trait he displayed. Terry was a very calm and peaceful manager; he always answered his phone and complimented us when we earned them. — Kenny W.

Bad bosses come in a lot of flavors. There's the absentee ones, who hide in the back and don't show up for much of anything besides performance appraisals, quietly cashing bonus checks. There's the indecisive ones, who will be upset if they aren't included in a decision-making process but will passive-aggressively suggest you be more self-motivated

when you do try to include them. There's the micro-
management sort, who won't let you be long enough to
actually do any work while they tell you how they think you
should sweep a floor or staple a document.

There are the chummy ones, the ones who can't seem to
hold the reins of authority because they're too concerned
with being everyone's buddy, or the opposite of that one,
just the downright jerks.

Good bosses, but in contrast, don't really come in that many
flavors. They're just the good ones. The ones who manage to
toe the line between all the perilous pitfalls on all sides of
them. And I'm here to tell you, Terry has the best balance of
anyone I've ever worked for.

He was brought into our store as a kind of fixer.

We had been without a manager for a while, and the store
had started to list under the direction of our two assistant
managers, one of whom had gone a little rotten without any
authority over him. I didn't quite feel at liberty to voice
some of my concerns to Terry when he first arrived. With
the backstage politicking of a workplace, I was worried
something said in confidence might make its way back to
our AM, and if he had stayed on, it would have made things
very awkward. So I had to just kind of stay quiet, keep my
head down, and hope that Terry was good enough to catch
what was going on.

Lucky for me and for our store, that trust was not misplaced.
Terry was able to suss out the problem and deal with it. I
didn't get to make his job any easier there in the beginning,
and I'm sorry for that. He never lost that trust, either. You
could always count on him to have your back, and he'd
always be fair. That kind of feeling is a great comfort in the
workplace. — Nathan K.

Terry is a leader that cares and has a good heart. He knows you have to lead by example and have a good relationship with all you lead. Terry taught me quite a bit about how to be a leader. I'm very thankful that he has come into my life. — Kammy C.

Terry's way of managing had a certain quality that I think often goes unnoticed; he had the unique ability to know when to be hands-on and jump in to help and when to sit back and let his people self-manage. It may not sound like much, but anybody who's had a supervisor who's hard to track down and get help from or talk to, or conversely one that hovers over you and suffocates your clarity and workflow, will appreciate that balance he strikes every day. — Lucas G.

Working with Terry - If I had to use one word to explain working with Terry, I would use beneficial. Terry was a very hardworking manager. I appreciated the time I had under his supervision. He was very honest and professional and had great communication skills. His work ethic was amazing, and he made sure to reach all the goals that were given to us. I am grateful to have had experienced a leader like him. — Koria A.

When Terry first came to my store, I was nervous. I was so used to my first mgr... To my great relief, I had a great manager and very good friend. Love You Boss. — Mitchell T.